Everyone's Guide to the
Bullmastiff

By Carol Beans

REVODANA PUBLISHING

REVODANA PUBLISHING

81 Lafayette Avenue, Sea Cliff, N.Y. 11579

Copyright © 2017 Revodana Publishing

All rights reserved

ISBN: 978-1-943824-37-3

Without limiting the rights under copyright reserved above, no part of this publication may be reproduced, stored in or introduced into a retrieval system, or transmitted, in any form or by any means (electronic, mechanical, photocopying, recording or otherwise), without the prior written permission of the publisher.

The scanning, uploading and distribution of this book via the Internet or via any other means without the permission of the publisher is illegal.

www.revodanapublishing.com

Cover photo: Gail Painter

Table of Contents

1. History of the Breed 5
2. AKC Breed Standard 11
3. Temperament and Character 15
4. Gait and Movement 21
5. Breeder and Buyer Responsibilities 25
6. How to Choose a Puppy 33
7. Bringing Up Baby 43
8. Health and Wellness 55
9. Showing Your Bullmastiff 67
10. Obedience Training 77
11. Breeding Bullmastiffs 83
12. The Stud Dog and Brood Bitch 89
13. The Babies 101
14. Spaying and Neutering 121
15. The Late Years to Goodbye 125

Glossary 129

Outstanding Bullmastiffs and Their Pedigrees 132

Farcroft Felon Frayeur, born 1927, an early U.K. champion

Chapter 1

History of the Breed

The Bullmastiff was developed in the Midlands of England, and was accepted by the country's kennel club as a purebred in 1924. However, its development began many years before. Bulldog and Mastiff crosses have been referred to in publications as early as the mid-1800s.

Born in the early 1900s, Thorneywood Terror weighed only 90 pounds. But he was undefeated when paired against any would-be assailant.

Previously, dogs of this type had been called Gamekeeper's Night Dogs, or Keeper's Night Dogs. Gamekeepers on England's vast estates needed help protecting the estates' game from poachers who trespassed on the land and illegally hunted deer, rabbit and game birds. The gamekeeper definitely needed help in patrolling the forests and meadows of the preserve. At one time, poaching was a capital offense. (Poachers were also often "transported." Usually they were sent to Australia, never to see their families again.) Therefore, the gamekeeper's life could be in danger with a poacher, since the man could not be hung any higher for killing the keeper than he would be for stealing a rabbit.

The Gamekeepers Night Dog – the Bullmastiff – was the answer to the problem. He was the perfect combination of his ancestors, the Old English Mastiff and the English Bulldog. (The English Bulldog of the 19th Century was longer legged and far more agile than the present-day representative of the breed.) While the Mastiff was certainly large and powerful enough to do the job, he did not have the agility and speed required. The Bulldog of that day had plenty of speed and agility, but was far too ferocious. The combination of the two breeds produced a dog that was powerful, agile,

GUIDE TO THE BULLMASTIFF

fearless and yet manageable.

The method used by the Bullmastiff to capture the poacher was to knock him down and keep him down until the gamekeeper came and took the poacher into custody. The Bullmastiff was also capable of dispatching the large and often ferocious hunting dogs accompanying the poachers.

Since most poaching was done at night, the gamekeepers preferred a dog whose coloring would blend into the surroundings. Brindle was the original preferred color of the breed for that reason.

In 1900, at the first Gamekeepers Dog Show, William Burton demonstrated the ability of these dogs to down and hold by offering £1 to anyone who could withstand his Thorneywood Terror's attempt to bring him down and keep him there. Terror was a 90-pound brindle who was securely muzzled during the contest. The dog never lost.

Prior to World War I, there were a number of breeding programs developing the Bullmastiff. There is some thought that breeds other than Mastiff and Bulldog were employed in the breedings at that time. The breed had not yet been recognized by the United Kingdom's Kennel Club, and the important factor was developing a dog to do a specific job.

Above: **Early Bullmastiff Tigers Vindictive.**
Below: **Beauty of Bulmas, 1950s.**

Sir James and Lady Dunn and their Bullmastiff, U.K., 1934.

In the early part of the 1920s, Sam Mosely began the most systematic breeding program of the period with Bulldogs and Mastiffs to set a type. He developed a dog whose characteristics were 60 percent Mastiff and 40 percent Bulldog. Many of his first Bullmastiffs bore the Hamil prefix, although he is famous for his Farcroft Bullmastiffs. It is believed that all modern Bullmastiffs descend from his stock.

Farcroft Fidelity, a fawn dog, was the first Bullmastiff eligible for the Kennel Club Stud Book, and the first Bullmastiff to win a first prize at a Kennel Club show. Farcroft dogs were very prominent in the list of winning show dogs in the decade following the breed's recognition.

In 1925, the Midland Bullmastiff Club established a standard for the Bull-Mastiff (the spelling used for the breed until about 60 years ago). The height of the breed at that time was an inch less at the shoulder for dogs and bitches than the present American standard. The dogs and bitches were also described as about 20 pounds lighter in weight than their present-day counterparts.

Fawns and reds were now popular colors in the breed, and as time progressed the brindle took a back seat to these in popularity, to the point that the color was almost lost. Mr. and Mrs. Warren of Harbex Kennels were the dominant force in keeping the color in the breed.

Pioneers who helped establish the breed include Mr. Burton (Thorneywood), Mr. Biggs (Osmaston), Mr. Barrowcliffe (Parkvale), Mr. Sam Moseley (Farcroft), Mr. Victor Smith (Pridzor), Mrs. Doris Mullin (Mulorna), Dorothy Nash (Le Tasyll), Mr. and Mrs. Higginson (Stanfell), Mr. and Mrs. Warren (Harbex) and Mr. Cyril Leeke (Bulmas). These are but a few well-known names of many who devoted themselves to the Bullmastiff.

Ch. Roger of the Fenns, born in 1929, is in the pedigree of every Bullmastiff alive today.

Some early dogs well known to breed enthusiasts are Ch. Tiger Prince (first Bullmastiff champion), Ch. Roger of The Fenns, Ch. Tenz, Ch. Athos, Ch. Farcroft Finality, Ch. Simba, Ch. Jeannie of Wyland, Ch. Wendy of Bulmas, Ch. Billy of Bulmas, Ch. Bubbles, Ch. Springwell Major and Ch. Rosalind Felice, to name a few.

The future of the breed rests with the dedicated breeders all over the world who are continuing the careful and responsible breeding begun by these breed founders.

HISTORY OF THE BREED

Photo: Dan Hogan.

Chapter 2
AKC Breed Standard

General Appearance: That of a symmetrical animal, showing great strength, endurance, and alertness; powerfully built but active. The foundation breeding was 60 percent Mastiff and 40 percent Bulldog. The breed was developed in England by gamekeepers for protection against poachers.

Size, Proportion, Substance: Size - Dogs, 25 to 27 inches at the withers, and 110 to 130 pounds weight. Bitches, 24 to 26 inches at the withers, and 100 to 120 pounds weight. Other things being equal, the more substantial dog within these limits is favored. **Proportion** - The length from tip of breastbone to rear of thigh exceeds the height from withers to ground only slightly, resulting in a nearly square appearance.

Head: *Expression* - Keen, alert, and intelligent. ***Eyes*** - Dark and of medium size. ***Ears*** - V-shaped and carried close to the cheeks, set on wide and high, level with occiput and cheeks, giving a square appearance to the skull; darker in color than the body and medium in size. ***Skull*** - Large, with a fair amount of wrinkle when alert; broad, with cheeks well developed. Forehead flat. ***Stop*** - Moderate. ***Muzzle*** - Broad and deep; its length, in comparison with that of the entire head, approximately as 1 is to 3. Lack of foreface with nostrils set on top of muzzle is a reversion to the Bulldog and is very undesirable. A dark muzzle is preferable.

Nose - Black, with nostrils large and broad. Flews - Not too pendulous. ***Bite*** - Preferably level or slightly undershot. Canine teeth large and set wide apart.

Neck, Topline, Body: *Neck* - Slightly arched, of moderate length, very muscular, and almost equal in circumference to the skull. ***Topline*** - Straight and level between withers and loin. ***Body*** - Compact. Chest wide and deep, with ribs well sprung and well set down between the forelegs. Back - Short, giving the impression of a well balanced dog. ***Loin*** - Wide, muscular, and slightly arched, with fair depth of flank. ***Tail*** - Set on high, strong at the root, and tapering to the hocks. It may be straight or curved, but never carried hound fashion.

Forequarters: Shoulders - muscular but not loaded, and slightly sloping. Forelegs - straight,

GUIDE TO THE BULLMASTIFF

well boned, and set well apart; elbows turned neither in nor out. Pasterns straight, feet of medium size, with round toes well arched.

Pads thick and tough, nails black.

Hindquarters: Broad and muscular, with well-developed second thigh denoting power, but not cumbersome. Moderate angulation at hocks. Cowhocks and splay feet are serious faults.

Coat: Short and dense, giving good weather protection.

Color: Red, fawn, or brindle. Except for a very small white spot on the chest, white marking is considered a fault.

Promising fawn youngster. *Photo: Nina Paakkari.*

Gait: Free, smooth, and powerful. When viewed from the side, reach and drive indicate maximum use of the dog's moderate angulation. Back remains level and firm. Coming and going, the dog moves in a straight line. Feet tend to converge under the body, without crossing over, as speed increases. There is no twisting in or out at the joints.

Temperament: Fearless and confident yet docile. The dog combines the reliability, intelligence, and willingness to please required in a dependable family companion and protector.

Chapter 3

Temperament and Character

Most people choose a dog because they like its appearance. Far more important than appearance in day-to-day living with an animal is its temperament and behavioral tendencies.

The Bullmastiff came into existence as a companion and co-worker with the British gamekeeper. As previously mentioned, at the time of the development of the breed, protecting game preserves was a risky business. The gamekeeper needed a strong, agile, intelligent and obedient dog to assist him in his work and for his protection. The Gamekeeper's Night Dog, the forerunner of the Bullmastiff as we know it today, was just right for the job.

Bullmastiffs can be silly, but they also have a very serious side.

Not only does the Bullmastiff have all these characteristics, but he is also possessive and strong willed. He is not the dog for a person who will not combine affection with consistency and discipline. Remember in purchasing a Bullmastiff that this breed was developed as a *guard* dog. While a proper Bullmastiff is loving and friendly, he still has a strong instinct to try to control a situation. A dog is a pack animal. The family he lives with, and any other animals he lives with, are his pack. In every pack there must be a leader and a clearly established order of dominance (a pecking order). The dog must know his place to be comfortable in his surroundings and mentally secure in his status in life. The dog must *always* defer to all the members of the household and accept any friends welcomed by the family. The exception to this is that no dog should be subjected to teasing and ill treatment.

Children and guests should be clearly educated to the fact that the dog is a living, feeling creature, and not some sort of toy.

The Bullmastiff's combination of power, intelligence, strong will and devotion makes him a wonderful companion for someone looking for a dog with character. Life with a Bullmastiff is seldom dull. Control *must* be established by the owner from the *second* one takes possession of the dog.

Bullmastiffs make excellent companions and guards because in their minds *they own you*. They will try anything to get their own way. Males will generally try to force an issue or pout; females usually try the coy approach. ("If Daddy loved me, he'd let me do this.") Be forewarned. Once you have given a command or correction, stick to it. If you give in once, these dogs remember and will try to get away with the same thing a dozen more times. Corrections need only be as strong as the dog's behavior demands. With some Bullmastiffs, a strong "NO" is sufficient. Others need firmer methods. Start with the least severe correction. The Bullmastiff only needs to know you mean what you say. *Always be consistent.*

Another warning: When you correct your dog, you may find you have a budding Hamlet on your hands. The Bullmastiff has a very expressive face and will use this expressiveness to make you feel just terrible for breaking his little heart and disciplining him. Keep looking into those eyes and you will find yourself driven to begging forgiveness for doing exactly what you should have done.

The Bullmastiff with a proper temperament should not be aggressive and guardy all the time. The lovely thing about this breed is that the dogs have a "live and let live"

TEMPERAMENT AND CHARACTER

The forbidden chair: This stubborn Bullmastiff decided to snuggle there anyway.

attitude. Unless something is wrong, you should not see these dogs in their working mode. The Bullmastiff is perfectly content to watch TV with the family, sleep on his back with his feet in the air, play with family members or other family dogs, or just find his favorite spot to lie down where he can get a clear view of the goings-on in the house or yard. The Bullmastiff can go from lying perfectly still, completely at ease, to moving full speed in a matter of seconds. If something needs his attention, he'll be there. The Bullmastiff is very discriminating. He can tell who is legitimately on your property and who is trespassing. He knows the difference between someone you let into your house and someone trying to come through a window or over a fence.

The exception to that is the "spoiled dog." As I previously mentioned, the dog knows someone has to be in charge. If you let your dog have his way from infancy, never follow through on corrections, and make excuses for bad behavior, be aware that *you* have created a monster. In a breed this bright, strong willed and territorial, the dog will take over the decision-making process of who is welcome and who is not. This is a totally avoidable situation. Simply be sure everyone establishes their dominance over the dog in the pecking order. This is not saying to abuse the dog; simply take responsibility and follow through. A dog who is allowed to run amok at 20 pounds has no idea when he has grown to 120 pounds that he is one iota different than he was as a pup. If you don't want him on the couch as an adult, don't put him up there as a pup and then punish him when he gets older for what you trained him to do.

The Bullmastiff is a working dog, and as such should have good muscle tone and an alert mind. Mental stability is extremely important in a breed this size. In choosing a puppy for the average family situation, do not choose the most dominant, and certainly not one who is shy. Since the breed as a whole is strong willed, the puppy with the middle-of-the-road approach to life will be the most trainable and adaptable for a family situation.

Speaking of training, firm, consistent and kind training is a necessity. The Bullmastiff has a mind of his own and is far from stupid. You just need to convince the dog that even though he thinks his way of doing things is better than yours, you are paying for the dog food, so he's just going to have to humor you and do what you say.

The Bullmastiff is loyal and loving. He will give everything for those he loves. In return, it is only fair for the dog to receive respect and love from those with whom he lives.

Bullmastiffs come in three colors: Fawn, brindle and red, like this dog. While some owners might have preferences, all are equally correct according to the standard.

TEMPERAMENT AND CHARACTER

Photo: Theresa M. Lyons

Chapter 4

Gait and Movement

The breed standard outlines how the Bullmastiff should gait. Consider what the Bullmastiff was bred to do: "Form follows function." Everything about proper Bullmastiff structure lends itself to agility, strength and a good sense of balance.

The Bullmastiff is broad and deep in both the head and body. This gives him an excellent low center of gravity for balance. He can turn and dodge or be in full running stride in an instant. It is almost impossible to knock the dog off his feet. His strong, square skull is an ideal battering ram. His broad, strong underjaw makes an ideal gripping tool.

Unlike field dogs, hounds and herding dogs, the Bullmastiff was not required to travel long distances at a steady, ground-eating trot, so he doesn't need the lighter bone and acute angulation in the shoulder and rear assembly. The Bullmastiff standard calls for only moderate angulation in the hocks.

Balance and soundness require only moderate angulation at the stifle and the shoulder. More angulation in the rear than in the front would cause the dog to overreach. To prevent stepping all over the back of his front feet with his rear feet, a dog with this imbalance of angulation would either crab (offset the rear movement to one side so that the rear does not follow the same track as the front); try to shorten the rear stride, which causes a shuffling and unbalanced action; turn the hind feet out (giving a duck-like look to the rear movement), or exaggerate the front movement to avoid interference by the rear feet.

A dog that is more heavily angulated in the front than the rear has far more reach in the front and little help from the rear in propelling the dog forward. Instead of a smooth, even gait, this problem produces a dog who appears to be dragging his rear along as an afterthought rather than using it to equal benefit. Just as the dog who is lacking in front angulation may shorten the rear stride to compensate, the dog who is more angulated in the front may tend to shorten his front reach, again producing an inefficient gait.

The key word in movement in a working dog is *efficient*. What is efficient in one breed is not in another. Gait fits structure, structure fits the purpose for which the dog was developed. Efficient movement propels a dog forward with the least exertion and wasted motion.

Since the Bullmastiff is broad and deep in body, it would be unreasonable to demand the dog to single track (every foot falling on the same central line under the body when moving forward at the trot). However, wide movement (trotting on two widely spaced parallel tracks) gives the dog a most inefficient, rolling gait. Proper, efficient movement for the structure of the Bullmastiff is one in which the legs move forward with reach and drive suited to the balanced, moderate angulation, converging forward a center line under the dog's body. The faster the dog is trotting, the closer the feet converge toward that center line. The hocks should not point in or wobble from side to side when the dog is trotting, and the stifle and/or lower hind legs should not turn outward. The elbows and/or pasterns should not rotate inward or outward, causing either a paddling or pigeon-toed gait in front.

The Bullmastiff's gait should denote power. Mincing, shuffling, rolling gaits are all seriously faulty movement because they are inefficient. The dog should travel smoothly forward. The convergence at the trot should never be to the point of any of the feet crossing over that central line.

The standard calls for a short back. The back should also be firm. A loose, sagging back causes inefficient up-and-down motion of the spine, and interferes with proper coordination of the front and rear assemblies. The definition of "back" is the topline from the withers to the loin.

The Bullmastiff's primary work was not done at the trot. However, the dog still has to get from point A to point B. Proper structure and movement allow the dog to use as little energy as possible in doing so, conserving it for the job he is expected to do.

Chapter 5

Breeder and Buyer Responsibilities

The responsibilities relating to the purchase of a puppy lay on both sides of the transaction. This situation is a wonderful example of the Golden Rule: Think how you would feel if you were on the opposite side of the arrangement. How would you want to be treated?

Breeder Responsibilities

The responsibilities of the breeder start before the puppies are conceived. The dam should be current on all her vaccinations. She should be wormed and in good condition. She and the stud should be healthy, both mentally and physically.

The puppies should be raised in a clean whelping area. When they are weaned from their dam, they should have fresh water, good-quality food, room to exercise, be wormed and given all the necessary vaccines. They should be given affection and enough handling to have them be well socialized.

When people inquire about puppies, the breeder should answer all reasonable questions as clearly as possible. The breeder should be sure the prospective buyer understands all that goes into properly raising a healthy, happy, well-mannered dog.

The breeder should screen prospective buyers as carefully as possible to find out whether they can and/or will offer the puppy a safe and loving home.

The breeder has a responsibility to the breed to present the breed honestly, with all its virtues and flaws. There are no perfect dogs and no perfect kennels. Any breeder who downgrades other breeders' stock and glorifies only her own is doing no favor to the breed. An intelligent prospective buyer will eventually sort out the facts, and a bad impression made by one breeder may tarnish the buyer's image of the entire breed. A healthy, happy Bullmastiff puppy just about sells itself.

The breeder has the responsibility of giving the buyer the dog's registration certificate or registration application (explaining how to fill it out and file it with the American Kennel Club or other governing registry), a three-generation pedigree, a record of all previous vaccines and wormings, a schedule of vaccines and wormings due, a feeding schedule and diet plan, and any handy hints that can help the buyer simplify the puppy's adjustment to a new family and the family's adjustment to a new puppy.

The breeder should be sure the puppy is in good health before he leaves the property. A wise breeder will strongly suggest that a veterinarian check the puppy within 48 hours of purchase.

A responsible breeder will always be available to answer questions from his or her puppy buyers, within reason. Bullmastiffs are a unique breed. They do not always do things or react to things like other dogs. A breeder may know far better than a veterinarian what is normal for her own stock. Being available to a worried puppy owner has benefits far beyond the time spent.

A breeder has the responsibility to properly represent the quality of a puppy to the buyer. One can't always be right in deciding whether a puppy

Show quality or pet quality? The determination is a breeder's best guess — but a lot can change on the way to adulthood.

is show or pet quality. A puppy grows at a tremendous rate. Many changes can occur during the first year of growth. Some of these changes can be for the better, and others not. If a breeder sells a puppy as show quality and it emerges from the growth stage as something less than show quality, the responsible breeder will make some adjustment

BREEDER AND BUYER RESPONSIBILITIES

All breeders have an equal responsibility for maintaining stewardship of the breed.

with the buyer. There is no amount of a sales price that is worth the bad will of a buyer who feels he has been dealt with unfairly, and conversely a buyer who finds a breeder fair and helpful is the least expensive and best advertising a breeder can have.

Protect the breed by using limiting registration on pets and requiring spaying or neutering. If a breeder has a question as to whether a pup is just slow developing and may bloom by a year of age, the limited registration factor is a perfect control. It can only be lifted by the breeder. Limited registration prevents any offspring from the animal from being registered unless the breeder agrees to write to the AKC for a change of status.

Let's be clear on who a breeder is. Many people say, "I am not a breeder. I am just breeding this one litter." *Wrong!* When that litter is registered, there is a *breeder of record*. One litter, one puppy, can have a tremendous influence on a breed. Breeding is breeding. If one breeds once and produces a litter, that person has the exact same responsibilities to the breed and to the buyer as does the person who has been breeding for 20 years.

GUIDE TO THE BULLMASTIFF

Buyer Responsibilities

Although breeder responsibilities were defined first, buyer responsibilities are no less important. Given the fact that a buyer receives a healthy puppy from the breeder, what happens from that point on is on the buyer's shoulders. When one writes an email or phones or visits a breeder, that person should make his or her requirements clear and concise. State exactly what you are looking for (sex, color, show, pet). *Be honest!* If you think you think you may want to use the animal for breeding, *say so!* Do not shop for a pet-quality puppy for breeding purposes. Show- and breeding-quality pups make just the same kind of companions as pet-quality pups do. The proper reason for raising a litter is to attempt to improve with each generation. You will get what you pay for from a reputable breeder.

If you do just want a pet, don't be surprised if the breeder wants a neutering or spaying agreement as part of that sale. Be clear on what the terms of the sale are *before* you buy. Some breeders want you to sign agreements that the show-quality puppy that you buy from them will be shown. If you do not want to show, *don't* buy under these terms and complain later. If you are buying a bitch puppy, and the terms are that you must breed the animals and give a "X" number of puppies back to the person from whom you are buying the dog, compute the entire cost — price and puppies back — before you agree to buy.

If the breeder insists on being listed as co-owner of the pup, should the buyer pay full price for something he doesn't fully own? If the buyer agrees to co-ownership, for how long? Are expenses split? None of this may seem critical at the time you buy the puppy, but a year or two down the road that almost always changes. Have it clear in your mind just what you want. It is not fair to the buyer or breeder to make arrangements that one or the other has no intention of keeping. Don't believe that it doesn't matter what you

sign because you can always back out of it later. A contract is a contract!

When planning to visit a breeder, call ahead and arrange a specific time to visit. If you cannot keep the appointment, call and cancel. Most breeders have busy schedules; their time is valuable. Don't leave a breeder sitting around for hours waiting for someone who is not coming. Don't show up two hours early and expect to be welcomed.

Don't "kennel-hop." In other words, don't decide to visit two or three kennels or homes in one day.

Breeders don't need bacteria or viruses that may be lurking at someone else's place. Even though the other dogs may have developed an immunity, the next kennel's occupant may be wide open to whatever you are transferring.

If you bring children with you to see puppies at a home or kennel, *keep them under control*. If a prospective buyer's children spend the whole visit teasing or upsetting the breeder's dogs, it is unlikely the breeder will have much confidence that the buyer is capable of properly raising a Bullmastiff, or give one a safe or happy home.

The buyer should carefully inspect the puppy he wants to buy, checking both the physical condition and personality. It is unfair to the puppy and his breeder to wait until the pup gets to his new home and then have the new owner decide he really isn't wanted.

If you are buying a male pup for show and/or breeding purposes, check the pup to make sure both testicles are descended. Don't take the pup home, upset his routine and then bring him back.

It is a good idea for a prospective buyer to visit two or three breeders, if possible, before making up one's mind. It doesn't need to be done in a day. Seeing several litters, one becomes sure of the type one prefers, having gotten a good overview of what is available.

If, as a buyer, you have a definite preference for a puppy of a particular color or sex, it is wise to wait until that puppy becomes available. That way the buyer is sure to be satisfied, and the puppy is sure to be more appreciated by her new owner.

When you finally select a puppy, be sure to have all the proper paperwork and necessary health and feeding information before leaving the breeder's property. Take the puppy to a veterinarian for a check-up as soon as possible (within 48 hours), and have all the pertinent information you were given on hand to show the vet.

A reputable breeder will provide the knowledge and support you'll need to keep you afloat on your Bullmastiff adventure. *Photo: Lynne Klinger*

If you really like the looks and condition of the breeder's dogs, and the breeder has given you a schedule and diet for the puppy, *stick to it!* It is your responsibility as a buyer to do what is necessary for the best interests of the puppy. How you raise and feed and socialize your new puppy very strongly determines how he turns out.

Chapter 6

How to Choose a Puppy

So, you've decided to get a Bullmastiff puppy! Educate yourself before you buy. Be absolutely sure you understand what this breed is. And, for the puppy's sake, buy only what you really want. Puppies do know whether you are pleased with them.

Decide what sex, color, quality and personality you want in your puppy. Be sure to look at several litters or see pictures of several litters if the pup is coming from out of town. Feel really comfortable with your decision before you finalize anything.

Make a list of questions regarding things that are important to you. That way you won't forget what you want to know as soon as you see those cute little faces. It helps a breeder help you when you can explain clearly what you are looking for. Do not get talked into taking something you had no intention of buying because it is all that is left and you don't want to wait another week or month or several months. This dog will be a part of your household and will hopefully live with you for nine years or more. A month or two is no time at all compared to the length of time you will own the dog.

Some breeders identify their puppies by the color ribbon they assign them at birth. More important than color, though, are the preferences you have for your new puppy.

Before you take up your time and a breeder's time with a visit, ask a few questions on the phone to make sure that there is a chance that this trip to see the pups has some possibility of success. Ask for a description of the parents, their health, temperament, etc. Find out if the breeder has available the quality (pet or show), the color and the gender you are looking for before you go see the litter. Find out the price range of the pet and show-quality puppies. Not all breeders charge the same prices. Find out what the breeder's position is on guarantees. Find out if there is a sales contract. If you are really interested in the litter, it might be a good idea to have a copy of the contract sent to you before you see the pups. Read the fine print. Understand what is required of you and what is required of the breeder. If you question anything you are told and the seller says, "Everyone does this," that is a bad sign. Every breeder sets his or her own standard of business, and few if any do exactly the same as another.

If you are willing to sign a contract, prepare to live up to it. Not all breeders have contracts, and not all contracts are the same. You might have to place a deposit on a puppy before you can visit the litter. Many breeders have waiting lists. Be sure there is an understanding that the deposit is refundable. However, if you do make a deposit and change your mind, the breeder may hold that deposit until the pup is sold.

Don't expect to be allowed to see very young puppies. Visits from outsiders can upset the brood bitch. At any early age, the pups can't be handled by outsiders for fear of stress and spreading viruses and bacteria. Better to arrange to visit when the pups are about six weeks old, out and about, and ready to visit.

When you finally get to see a litter, try to stand back and observe the litter before the pups see you. Watch how they interact with each other. If the breeder allows you to visit the whole litter, find out which puppies are available before you get your heart set on one that isn't. In fact, you should be allowed to see every available puppy that meets your requirements. Approach quietly and watch the puppies' reaction to you. If they appear to be just observing in an interested manner, or come to greet you, these are both normal reactions. Try to choose a puppy who starts forward, stops to give you a good look (remember the pups are deciding if they like you, too) and then comes to visit. This is very likely a very intelligent, tractable dog.

Look at the condition of the puppies and their surroundings. A place doesn't have to be a palace, but it should be clean and the pups in good condition. Fat is not fit. Sometimes it is difficult to control the piglets in the litter when they are all eating out of one dish. The pups should have their ribs well covered; their coats should be in good, shiny condition. Puppies with their ribs showing all over and their bellies swollen are very likely suffering from an infestation of intestinal parasites. By the age of six to eight weeks, they should be steady in their movement and sure on their feet, They should be interested in their surroundings unless you show up at nap time. Try to arrive a little while before a feeding. After a meal, the babies sort of drift off.

To most people, all Bullmastiff puppies are adorable. Remember what you wanted before you saw the litter? Think about it while you are looking at the litter.

If you are shopping for a pet puppy, remember as a member of your family this puppy's general health, temperament and personality are highly important. Most breeders sell as pets puppies that carry too much white, are not quite as heavy boned as the show quality, don't have quite the strength of skull, have eyes that are light, do not have a dark mask, are not quite as angulated as a show and breeding quality puppy. None of these things have a negative effect on a dog being an excellent, healthy pet. You and the breeder may be surprised, as some of these pups may be late bloomers. No matter the outward appearance, most Bullmastiffs are all the same inside. They have the same intelligence and ability to give undying affection, and to think of wicked things to do to get your attention. The wrapper may be a little different, but the contents are the same.

If you are looking for a pet rather than a show dog, if you have small children, if either adult in the household is a non-assertive person, *do not* choose the most dominant puppy in the litter. It won't work out. Also, do not choose a puppy that shows real fear of you. Some pups are reserved and wait a while to come forward. The important thing

is that they come forward to you on their own accord.

If the pet puppy is to go into an adult household and the owners are both assertive people, a dominant-natured puppy can be a wonderful experience, and lots of fun. These little darlings will test your will to govern for a bit, but if you are consistent you can have a terrific relationship with this type of dog. They are the ones who are born to be pack leaders, but properly trained, will be the exceptional dogs. If you cannot say "NO," and mean it, don't get one of these. But if you are used to large, working-breed dogs and mean what you say, you'll love living with this type. It is definitely not for everyone.

The breeder will probably give you an opinion on the qualities and temperament of each puppy. Do not be surprised if a breeder tells you a certain puppy would not do well in your household. Don't take it as an insult. Be thankful. The breeder should know her own dogs. Matching a puppy to prospective owners' lifestyles and personalities is important. Remember, all this pet dog is meant to do is live with you, love you, fit into your household, be your companion. Making the proper match is important.

To be honest, all Bullmastiff puppies are cute. Your breeder will help match you to the puppy with the best personality for your lifestyle.

In choosing a puppy for future showing and breeding, there are a number of other points to consider. You still need to consider the temperament and personality and general health. But now you are going to have to be aware of the finer points of the breed. It is very wise to have carefully read the breed standard before looking at puppies to buy. (See page 11.) Puppies will not exactly fit the standard but at the age they are ready to leave home, one should be able to see basic structure, get a really good idea of soundness in movement, and understand the temperament. Puppies' temperaments are not made. They are born with them. Personalities and behavior can be worked with. A dominant temperament is a dominant temperament. A passive is a passive. That doesn't change. How you raise and train a pup can control the temperament to a degree and mold the personality. Neither dominant nor passive is bad. These temperaments need to be settled in the right homes with the right people.

In choosing a show-quality puppy, you need to look for the correct *type*. Correct type is what is described in the breed standard. The breed standard is a description of perfection for the breed. No dog is perfect. The best dogs have the fewest and least deviations from the standard. Look for balance. Is the dog equally angulated in shoulders and rear quarters? Is the back strong and level? Is the chest deep and broad? Are the front legs straight from body to top of the feet, with no inward or outward turn at the ankle? Are the hindquarters broad, with good second-thigh development? Beware of splayed feet. The toes should be thick and well arched. Does the dog have substantial bone structure? Is the skull square and the muzzle a smaller, matching square in appearance? Are the eyes dark, the nose leather black, the nostrils large and open wide, the mask dark, and the ears darker than the body?

Check the teeth and jaws. At the age of eight weeks, a puppy may have a scissors bite (top teeth just sliding over the bottom teeth), or level, or very slightly undershot. If a puppy is already very undershot, you can count on the mouth not getting any better, and probably getting worse. The bottom jaw grows after the upper jaw stops, so if a dog has a scissors bite it can go level to slightly undershot. A level bite can stay that way or go under. Watch out for wry mouth (lower jaw length longer on one side than the other) and a pup with the defect is not a show or breeding animal. A mouth can go wry as late as six months. Sometimes eyes that are a bit light will darken. Very light eyes will seldom darken enough to be correct.

As with this brindle youngster, ears should be set level with the top of the skull.

Puppies can have very large ears at this age. They often grow into them, though it seems like forever before they do. Very small ears will stay that way, in my experience. The ears should be set on level with the top of the skull. Low-set ears give the skull an "apple-headed" appearance and very high-set ears spoil the balance of the head. During the teething stage, the puppy may fold his ears back and carry them high. That usually corrects itself when the teething pain ceases and also when the back skull spreads with maturity.

Is the coat color pure and clear? If you see a black overlay on the puppy, it more than likely will clear in a few months, or by the time the dog is a year. It may remain in some cases. Some dogs have a very washed-out appearance around the cheeks, chest, underside, inside of the legs and the buttocks. This two-toned appearance does not go away. As for color, that is your own choice. Brindle, red and fawn are all proper colors. Some fairly large white spots on the chest will reduce in size as the pup grows. Many will not. A large white bib or a wide blaze will not go away. Toes that are wholly white will not fill in. Small white marks on toes can, and often do, fill in. White on the face seldom, if ever, goes away.

Brindle is a dominant trait, so one parent must be "stripey" in order for the offspring to be.

A puppy with ice-blue eyes, and a red or blue mask, is not going to be a show dog. The eyes will eventually turn yellow. These dogs are calls Dudleys. They have a genetic dilute pigmentation factor. They make fine pets, but are definitely not for show or breeding. Pass them over if you are looking for a show or breeding prospect. Puppies with silky coats (a very noticeable difference in coat textures, with little fringes on ears and limbs) that are obviously longer than normal are probably long hairs, some say a genetic throwback to the Tibetan Mastiff ancestors of all Mastiff breeds, and who knows what from the early developmental stage from the breed. Pass them up except for pets as well.

Some puppies have light toenails when they are born. Some stay white, and in others the nails start to darken at around six weeks. If you see white nails on a pup, pull back the hair where the nail enters the toe to see if there is a dark pigmentation coming in. Although the standard calls for black nails, if the worst you can find wrong with a pup are a few white toenails, don't worry about it.

The puppy should be able to trot squarely. Most pups at this age like to bounce around and gallop all over the place. Take the pup away from the others where it will not be distracted and it will probably trot. If the surface is good, the puppy should be sure on her feet. She should move with assurance and balance. A puppy who is a stunning mover at six to eight weeks, barring some tragedy, will stay that way. An eight-week-old pup that is really unsteady is not very likely to be a good show prospect.

A puppy with beautiful type and movement still must have a good temperament. No matter how good a show dog, it must still live with someone.

Temperament is important. The puppy should be outgoing, interested and attentive to you. This applies to both pet and show stock.

If you are visiting a litter and have any reservations about a puppy being the right one for you, do not hesitate to go home and think about it overnight. It is very hard to make a rational decision with the darling puppies staring into your eyes. If you have travelled a long distance and don't want to go all the way home to think it over, go to a restaurant or a park or just anywhere away from the property where the pups are, and think about your decision or discuss it. A half-hour, an hour, a day will give you some perspective. A breeder should not object to you giving this decision careful thought. This is a major investment, and it isn't every day you can buy unquestioning love.

Chapter 7

Bringing Up Baby

When a puppy comes home, the really important work begins. Actually, it began when the breeder placed the puppy in your hands. From that moment, it is your responsibility to create the pet you want.

Pet or show quality does not matter at this point. The basics will be the same, with the exception of the little extra training that it will take to train the dog for the show ring. The puppy is moving in with you, not vice versa. It must learn to adapt to your household and learn the house rules. Some of the following will help assure a puppy's growth into a happy, well-adjusted dog.

She's yours. Now what?

You are the pack leader, not the dog. The dog is a pack animal and fully understands pack psychology. Someone has to be in charge and if you won't take this responsibility, the majority of Bullmastiffs I have known will. The dog, like a small child, is most comfortable when there is consistency. He knows just how far it is safe to go. A dog who is not treated consistently will constantly test the borders of allowed behavior. A dog who knows what you want is comfortable and contented.

Do not let the dog do at 15 or 20 pounds what you don't want him to do at 120 pounds. The dog has no concept of growth. If it was fine when he was little, why shouldn't it be just as fine a year later?

If you give the dog a command, *follow through* — *never* decide that "just this once" the dog doesn't have to do what you want. To the dog it is not just this once, it is your pattern of operation. If he got away with it this time, he will ignore you the next time, too. You will probably have to prove your point a dozen times once you let a Bullmastiff sidestep an order once.

"NO" means "NO." Do not say, "No," and then just let the matter slide. This means no matter how sad or insulted the puppy gets at being told, "No," that is still what you mean and the order stands. You have never seen such marvelous acting as by a Bullmastiff trying to make you feel guilty. It's positively awe inspiring.

Praise a lot when the dog does what you want. Bullmastiffs live for it.

Give the puppy an area that is his from the very start, and in which he or she can be peaceful and unpestered. If you have children, they have a tendency to have their hands on the puppy all the time. A puppy is a baby and needs lots of sleep. A folding exercise pen or a nice large crate in a quiet corner is perfect for this purpose. For those unfamiliar with the wonders of a crate, this is not a torture chamber or a punishment. A dog is a den animal. In the wild it would dig a hole just big enough to fit into with sides close enough that nothing could get by her when he or she faced the entrance. The crate is the dog's den. It is a safe haven from noisy guests, overattentive children and the stresses of the day. It is a marvelous housebreaking tool. Feed your puppy in his crate and he will knock you down trying to get to it.

Be consistent with your housebreaking training. Confine the puppy when you are not watching him closely if he is in the house. If you are lucky enough to have good weather, it is good for the pup to be outside as much as possible. Free exercise is important to development. After you feed a puppy, take him right outside, either to a perfect spot, or if you don't care about that, to anywhere in the yard. Supervise the pup until he has urinated or defecated. Praise him grandly for doing what you wanted. If you wander around with him for a full five minutes, and he does nothing, take him back in the house, crate him and take him out 15 minutes later. If he accomplishes the purpose for which you took him out, he can then have some unconfined time in the house. A young puppy has to go often. Take him out every two hours when he's in the house. This does not mean every two hours after bedtime. Don't let the pup drink a large amount of water after eight or nine at night. Feed his last meal of the day by 7 or 7:30 p.m. Give him at least two outings after the meal. As the pup gets older, he will need to eliminate less often. By taking him out often, you get to know his schedule. *Do not give a puppy free run of the house unsupervised.* You may find unwanted gifts in the oddest places.

A puppy does not like to soil the area in which he sleeps. By confining the pup to that area when you are not watching him and taking him outside often, you are helping him control himself more easily.

Don't change foods all the time because you think the dog is bored with one kind. She isn't. Changing foods all the time upsets the dog's digestive system.

For the safety of your dog, a fenced yard is of optimum importance. There *must* be a fenced place for the dog outside if it she outside without a leash. This is a possessive, territorial breed. They like to believe they own everything. Remember what they were bred to do. Unfortunately, because they are large, no matter if some little dog comes up and bites them in the face, they don't respond without dire consequences for themselves and you. Nobody cares who started the altercation. Your dog is bigger, so in other people's minds, it is your dog's fault. Even a totally friendly Bullmastiff who decides to give some child on the sidewalk a big kiss will probably knock the child down in the process. The result — bills, bills, bills; a bad reputation for your dog and the breed, and then there's the neighbors' animosity. How much better to keep the dog where it belongs. Take him out on a leash where you can control his interaction with the public. Well-mannered Bullmastiffs are loved by the people who meet them under the right circumstances. There is also the possibility that an unfenced dog crosses the street at the wrong time or finds the neighbor's livestock irresistible. There are many negatives involved in letting one of these dogs run free.

A Bullmastiff should be socialized — get out to meet people and see new places as soon as his series of vaccines are complete. That is usually at four months of age. The more the pup sees early on, the easier he will adapt to new and changing things later. Socializing also includes learning the dog's place in each situation — what behavior is allowed and what isn't. When the pup was with his littermates, he tried any number of behaviors with them. The pup will quickly decide among the pups who could get away with what. Socialization is a normal but very important process.

While taking you puppy out to see the world, remember that she's just a baby. Puppies put everything they have into each thing they do, and tire easily. Their play periods are intense and short, and they need quiet time to nap or just rest in between. If you try to take a very young pup on a two-block walk, remember it's two blocks back, so think round trip. An over-tired puppy can pull a muscle or strain a ligament just that fast.

Make sure your puppy is well socialized. Expose him to well-mannered, friendly dogs of all breeds.

Realize that the bones, ligaments and muscles on a rapid-growing large-breed puppy do not grow at the same time. One day you may see the pup bumbling all over the place because he has had a growth spurt of ligamental tissue while the bones haven't caught up. Therefore, his bones have much less support. A couple of days later the bone growth can take off and pass the ligamental growth, and the pup's movement is stiff and restricted because of the pressure. I've explained to many new puppy buyers that you can go to bed one night and wake up the next morning, look at your puppy and swear she has visibly grown. People tend to laugh at that until they wake up one morning to a dog that is obviously bigger than he was the night before. Then I get the phone call telling me what I told them at the beginning. The one certain thing you can count on about your puppy in the first year is that he will change almost daily. Proper diet, managed exercise and realization that this is just a baby will ensure the best end result.

Who is this mysterious creature? Bullmastiff puppies go through all kinds of oddball growth spurts before settling into their real selves.

Bullmastiff puppies do grow in the most amazing ways. Some grow very slowly and evenly, but they are in the minority. Some shoot straight up and are all height and no width, and then broaden and fill out at the end of the growth stage. Others grow very slowly at first, making you think they are never going to get any height, and shoot up at the end of the growth stage. Most tend to grow rear end first. You wake up one morning and the hips are an inch or two taller than the top of the shoulders. Pretty soon the shoulders catch up and you breathe a sigh of relief. Not so fast! By the next week, the dog is walking downhill again. While the pup is this downhill stage it will probably trip himself, not know where any one foot is at any particular time, and generally make you embarrassed to let anyone see it. Where did that beautiful baby go? Will this misery ever end? Yes! Somewhere between a year and eighteen months, the ugly duckling turns into a swan. The dog will wake up and, lo and behold, everything fits just right! The girls tend to come together a little sooner than the boys.

Teething is a miserable stage for the pup. It usually starts just short of four months of age; some pups, a bit earlier. The pups can act like they have a terrible headache, which they probably do. They may carry their ears folded back because of the pain in their jaws. They may be a bit feverish, just as a human baby. They may not want to eat, because chewing really hurts. They will probably take to periods of chewing anything in their path. Putting a big rawhide or beef knuckle bone in the freezer for a while, and then giving it to the dog, can help ease some of the pain and help with the chewing stage. Some dogs go through this without major trauma. Others have terribly swollen gums; sometimes the swelling even extends into the face tissue. Make sure the puppy has the proper things to chew at this time. We've had some interestingly redesigned table and chair legs produced during this period in a pup's life. Make sure the first teeth come out as the second set comes in. On rare occasions, dogs will try to retain the first set. This can put the bite alignment off. Your early training for your show prospect to allow the mouth to be examined is invaluable at this time.

Teach your dog manners. You may not mind the dog leaping all over you, but I can guarantee that almost everyone else will hate your dog for it.

When you bring the puppy home, have her own quiet area prepared. Have some toys on hand, have the proper food already at the house. Do not stop at all your friends' and relatives' homes first so they can admire the baby. This is a *huge* change in the puppy's life. Make it as smooth as possible. Give the puppy a chance to eliminate. Give her a small amount of water. If it is feeding time, give her about two-thirds to three-fourths of her normal meal. If the pup eats, take her out to eliminate. Confine the puppy to a small area, preferably her own quiet area, for a little nap. After the pup has rested, she can be taken outside for another potty stop, and then played with for a while. Most puppies adapt quite easily.

The real message of who is running the show comes at bedtime the first night. Most puppies have slept in a whelping box or a pen with their littermates. They have not slept in bed with their owners. Of course, a puppy who has had several littermates to sleep with will be lonely at first. But going to sleep in her crate or pen is one of the first steps in learning to adapt to your house. Give the puppy a large, plush toy animal to sleep with. They are readily available in pet stores. Give the pup a Nylonbone or large chew toy. (*No squeakers inside* — they eat them and you get a big vet bill for your kindness.) Put a radio on low volume in the same room with the pup if you think the sound of voices or music will ease the way. It is very likely the pup will do some whimpering, even some serious howling. Unless you really believe the pup needs to go out to eliminate, *don't* go see what is going on. That is the first step in training you to do what the dog wants. There is a vast difference between the sound of a puppy whimpering, having a little tantrum, and real need. Learn the difference. If the pup learns the first night that she has to stay where she has been put, and you will greet her lovingly in the morning, you likely will not have to go through the same dance the next night. I've never had a pup require more than two nights to get the message. If you are extremely lucky, your pup will curl up and pass out and you won't hear from her until first thing in the morning, when it is definitely a good idea to get the pup fast and get her outside. The later you make the last outing at night before bedtime, the better the chances of getting through the night.

The breeder probably gave you feeding, vaccine and worming schedules. As I've said before, if you like the condition of the breeder's dogs, follow those schedules.

You should take the puppy to your vet for an initial check-up within the first 48 hours after bringing her home. When you go to the vet's office, *do not* put the puppy down on the floor. No matter how clean the office is, there have been sick dogs there with diseases that you probably have never heard of. In a crate, in your arms or on an examination table are the only places the pup should be on this trip.

Be sure the vaccination program includes distemper, canine hepatitis, parvovirus, bordetella nasal vaccine (kennel cough) and in some areas leptospirosis and Lyme disease vaccine, depending on your vet's recommendation. At four months in most states, the pup needs a rabies vaccine. When you bring the pup home from a trip to the vet for vaccines, give him plenty of quiet time that day. Remember what vaccines are: a small dose of the disease that the dog's system must gear up to fight off.

Take a stool sample to the vet on the first trip. He can check it for any parasites that might need to be treated.

Beware of toys with squeakers: They can have an unhappy ending.

Feed the puppy on schedule, generally three times a day until about four months. After that, twice a day is good. The pup may start leaving his midday meal earlier. You can drop that meal if the pup rejects it three days in a row and is showing no signs of ill health that would affect his appetite. Don't decrease the amount of food; just split it into two meals. Some people continue a twice-a-day feeding schedule for the life of the dog. Others, after a dog is a year of age, reduce the feeding to once a day, with a nice dog biscuit in the morning. You will gradually increase the amount of dry food as the pup grows. At five to 10 months of age, the dog will require more food than when he reaches 12 to 15 months of age. A mature dog needs less food for maintenance than a pup needs for growth. Adjust the food quantity by observing your dog's appearance. If the dog appears a little thin, add a half-cup or a cup of dry food per day. Some growing males just never seem to carry enough weight, until they reach a year of age. If they are healthy in all other respects, and you are feeding them plenty, don't worry about it. If the dog appears a little bit on the heavy side, take away a half-cup or a cup of food each day. If you can't stand the Academy Award-winning, hopeless look of the dog who wants more, you can substitute cooked, canned green beans or cooked rice for a cup of food — almost no calories, and filling at the same time. You want to keep the pup in good condition, so you need only enough to keep a nice, tight covering of flesh over the ribs. You don't want the dog skinny, but you want him to look fit. A little canned food in the dry food is fine. Remember, canned food is largely water, and dry food is a complete and balanced diet. I use a small amount of canned food and a cup of water mixed with dry food.

Supplements, despite the advertising campaigns, are not the best thing for large-breed dogs. A good dry dog food that states it is a complete diet is just that. Extra vitamins and minerals can force growth. Forced growth causes the growth plates at the end of the long bones to calcify too soon, leaving gaps in the joints, which then slip or rub, and cause arthritis and pain and other problems you don't want to deal with. Vitamin E and vitamin C are both acceptable. The first is an antioxidant, and the second is beneficial in the development of collagen, which strengthens bones, cartilage and muscle tissue. Vitamin C is water soluble, so if you feed too much, it is released from the system as it builds up in the body if overused.

Adding table scraps to a dog's meal is fine occasionally, but should never be a regular thing. A dog's dry food is properly balanced; adding a lot of extras changes that balance. Giving a dog a cookie or two a day is just fine. Just realize it has food value, and adjust the diet accordingly.

If you want a floor instead of a water slide, keep your dog's water dish outside. They never seem to finish the last mouthful. If the weather is good, this is easy. If a dog is confined to the house for long hours, you will need an inside dish. I've noticed the Bullmastiffs love to hold that last mouthful of water until they can walk right up to you, open their mouths, and leave most of the last mouthful on your shoes and clothes.

Giving them an outside dish and letting them back in five minutes after they've finished drinking cures the problem for those of us who don't live to do laundry. Your dog should have water available for most of the hours of each day.

Trim your puppy's nails on a regular basis. It's a lot easier convincing a little one to stand still for this than waiting until he weighs almost as much as you do, and considers his toenails off limits. Get the puppy used to having his ears checked, too. Use a soft, barely damp cloth to clean the easily reachable surfaces.

Early on, your Bullmastiff puppy should learn routine procedures like nail trimming.

Give the puppy a good brushing once a week. This is good for the skin and circulation, and is another method of bonding with your pup. Whether or not your dog is going to be just a family companion or a family companion and show dog combined, it is a good idea to start the dog in a basic obedience class at six months of age. It's good socialization. It will also give you the tools and control you need to make your dog a pleasure to live with. All adult members of the household should participate in this training, even the older children if they have an interest in doing so. The dog should behave for everyone in the household, and everyone in the household should be educated on how to ensure the dog obeys them. Actual obedience to your rules should have started the second you acquired the dog.

If you follow a good feeding regimen, keep the pup in good condition, don't overstress the growing pup, give him basic training, lots of love and consistent rules, and have a little faith, you will come through the baby and growth stage with a wonderful friend and a Bullmastiff to be proud of.

BRINGING UP BABY

Photo: Lynne Klinger

Chapter 8

Health and Wellness

The most important decision you will make after selecting your puppy is selecting your veterinarian. Choose carefully! If you do not already have a veterinarian with whom you are totally satisfied, start looking for one. Remember, the veterinarian works for you and your dog — not the other way around.

The fanciest office is not an indication of the ability of the veterinarian occupying it. Discuss fees — the most expensive treatment is not always the best treatment. On the other hand, don't choose a vet because he is the least expensive. You want someone who is competent, caring, *who will listen to you*, who will take the time to explain a situation fully, who will be available when needed, and with whom *you feel comfortable*.

Look for someone who starts with the simplest, most logical, basic approach to a problem. If a problem is life threatening, it is very likely to be obvious to you, too. For less serious problems, many times, good, basic common-sense treatment is all that is necessary. You can always increase your efforts in treating a dog, but it is not necessary to start out with the most extreme treatment, unless the dog is in acute trouble. In other words, brain surgery is not necessary for a cut on the head.

Be forewarned: If your puppy is for breeding purposes in the future, find a veterinarian who has a number of breeders as clients. Established breeders do not stay with someone who does not fill their needs. Not all vets are interested in dealing with breeding animals, and the extra knowledge and time required as compared to a pet animal. If your puppy is to be solely a pet, you still need a vet who will fulfill the criteria mentioned earlier.

Many veterinarians suggest feeding regimens for a new puppy. If you get a puppy from an established breeder, that person will probably give you a diet plan and feeding schedule. If you like the condition of the breeder's dogs and the puppies you have seen at the breeder's home, it is probably wise to show the diet plan to your veterinarian and explain that you wish to follow it. If you have not received such information from the seller of your puppy, you may follow the suggestions outlined in this booklet, or ask your vet for suggestions. Bullmastiffs are different from many other dogs, so what is good for the general dog population is not always good for dealing with the Bullmastiff.

Do keep in mind that, in the main, Bullmastiff puppies do not do well with large doses of supplements. Forcing growth can cause a lot of structural problems.

If you live near the breeder of your puppy, you may want to use the same veterinarian. The veterinarian is probably very familiar with the breed, having the advantage of treating the breeder's dogs.

Establish a vaccine and worming schedule with your vet, and follow it. If the breeder has given you a vaccine and worming schedule, you may want to use that one.

When you visit the vet's office with your dog, write all your questions down in advance so you can save time and be organized. If you do not understand something you are told, or if you want a diagnosis or direction explained, ask the vet to do so. Do not leave the office without fully understanding the diagnosis, treatment and dosage instructions on any medication.

Bullmastiffs are stoic: If they are in pain, most won't let on.

Bullmastiffs are stoic. They hate to give in to pain. *Learn to read your dog's expression and body language.* A Bullmastiff can appear normal to the casual glance and still be very ill. If you feel there is really something wrong with your dog, take her to the vet and insist on a thorough check-up. Sometimes you will see symptoms of illness a day or two before they become obvious to someone who is not familiar with the dog's general attitude and daily activities.

When you receive a diagnosis of a problem from your vet, it is *your responsibility* as to what to do from that point on. If it not a life-threatening problem and you are

HEALTH AND WELLNESS

not prepared to make a snap decision, don't. Be sure of what course of action you want to take before you take it. Don't put off unpleasant necessities because they are unpleasant, but don't rush to judgment on procedures that, once done, cannot be undone.

The goal is a healthy, happy, active Bullmastiff.

A good veterinarian wants you to participate in the decision-making process.

In recent years, many advances in veterinary medicine have made some high-technology treatments and surgeries available for your dog. These procedures can be extremely expensive. Sometimes they are the only answers, and sometimes there are other, less extreme treatments that may very well work. If you are faced with the possibility of a procedure for your dog that starts in the thousand-dollar-and-up range, with the exception of a medical emergency, *get an independent second opinion*. Also talk to your breeder and any other knowledgeable dog people you know before proceeding. No good veterinarian will object to you getting an independent second opinion.

In summary, you and your vet are a team working for the best interests of your dog.

Competency, trust, responsibility and good communication are absolute necessities for a successful relationship between you and your veterinarian, and for the health and happiness of your dog.

Health Concerns

There are some health issues that are particularly associated with large breeds. The following discussion by Dr. Barbara Rreichel, DVM, focuses on those seen in Bullmastiffs. Starting out with a puppy from parents with a healthy genetic history and using common sense in raising your Bllmastiff can have an effect on his lifelong health.

Allergic Skin Disease

There are three principle types of allergic skin disease:

1) **Flea bite dermatitis** (FAD) – Severe sensitivity to flea saliva. In most areas, FAD is the most common cause of skin disease. Itching is the primary clinical sign and most often includes the tail base and back region. It is not uncommon to have coexistent allergies. Treatment is aimed at eliminating exposure to the flea. Other things, such as steroids, antihistamines and fatty-acid supplements, can help reduce the severe itching while flea control is being instituted.

2) **Atopy** – Considered to be due to an inherited tendency to develop a hypersensitivity to environmental allergens, such as grass, tree and weed pollens, and house dust. It can account for as much as 15 percent of allergies — second only to flea-bite dermatitis. Local environmental factors such as temperature, humidity and flora will influence the duration and severity of signs in an individual. Typical age of onset is between one and three years of age, with females having a slightly higher incidence of occurrence. Signs will usually worsen with age, and seasonal allergies may become non-seasonal.

Itching is the hallmark of atopy and usually involves the face, feet and abdomen. Other signs may include ear infections, skin infections, and greasy/flaky skin and coat. Avoiding offending allergens, if they have been identified, is best. Putting the dog on essential fatty acids may be beneficial as well. Steroids, antihistamines and medicated shampoos can all be used to help relieve the symptoms. Allergy testing is available so the offending allergens can be identified and hyposensitization can be done. This is successful in 60 to 70 percent of patients and can be beneficial (i.e., help reduce the need for other drug usage) in another 15 to 20 percent.

3) **Food hypersensitivity** – Food reactions are non-seasonal reactions caused by ingesting the offending food substance(s). Age of onset is variable, with no breed or sex predilection. It involves itching of any part of the body. Food allergies tend not to respond well to cortisone therapy. The most valid method of diagnosis for food allergies is to put the dog on a restricted test diet. Blood tests are also available to identify offending ingredients, but may not work as well as the elimination diets. Once an offending substance(s) is identified, avoidance is the key. It is also very likely that there will be concurrent allergies that will also need to be controlled.

Cardiomyopathy (Dilated)

Dilated cardiomyopathy (DCM) is common in dogs. Giant and large breed dogs are predisposed. A male predominance is reported in most breeds, but not all. It is strongly suspected that there is a genetic or heritable susceptibility, but it has not been proven. It can affect dogs as young as two years of age, but is most commonly seen between four and 10 years of age. The owners will usually notice signs such as weight loss, abdominal distention, sudden weakness, respiratory problems, exercise intolerance and anorexia. Most dogs can be treated on an outpatient basis. The doctor will do an EKG, X-rays, echocardiogram and bloodwork to see how severely affected the dog is. Then a treatment plan will be devised. There is no cure, so the treatment is designed to relieve the signs and make the dog comfortable. Sudden death can occur even if the dog is well controlled with medication. With good home care and regular veterinary attention, most dogs live for six to 12 months following the initial onset of heart disease.

Elbow Dysplasia

Elbow dysplasia is a general term that describes four developmental abnormalities that lead to malformation and degeneration of the elbow joint. Elbow dysplasia is an inherited disease, and heritability is high. Elbow dysplasia is one of the most common causes of forelimb lameness in large-breed dogs. Typical age of onset is four to 10 months. Signs related to degenerative joint disease (DJD) can occur at any age. Feeding a high-calorie, high-protein diet that produces rapid weight gain will increase the incidence of the disease. On physical exam, the veterinarian can usually elicit some pain from the affected elbow, but X-rays may be necessary to diagnose elbow dysplasia. Surgery is the recommended treatment. Severity of accompanying DJD and the age of the dog can influence how successful the surgery will be. Breeding of affected animals should be discouraged, and breedings that result in offspring with elbow dysplasia should not be repeated with the same sire and dam.

Persistently chewing feet or licking between toes can be a sign of allergies.

Peek-a-boo! Bullmastiffs are very athletic, and need to be orthopedically sound.

Entropion

Entropion is a conformational defect in which the eyelid turns inward. The lower eyelid is more often affected. You may notice that the dog has a chronic discharge in the affected eye(s). Sometimes, you can even see the lower eyelashes rubbing on the eye if the lid is turned in a great deal. The way to correct the problem is to surgically remove the excessive tissue, so that the affected eyelid does not turn onto the surface of the eye anymore.

Hip Dysplasia

Hip dysplasia is the most prevalent disorder of the canine hip and the most significant cause of osteoarthritis in that joint. It affects large and giant breeds as early as four months. The dog's hip is a ball-and-socket-type joint. With dysplasia, the ball fits poorly into the socket and causes excessive wear and tear on the joint. The scraping of the cartilage can cause varying degrees of pain. It has been shown that there is a complicated polygenetic transmission of the disease. The expression of the disease can be determined by an interaction of genetic and environmental factors. When the genetic potential for dysplasia is present, feeding a high-calorie, high-protein diet that produces rapid weight gain will increase the incidence and severity of the disease.

Hind-leg lameness, swaying or staggering, discomfort upon rising, and reluctance to run and jump are all symptoms of hip dysplasia. X-ray examination is the only way to accurately diagnose dysplasia. Mild cases may not show up on X-rays until the age of two years. A "dysplasia free" certification cannot be given until that age. Hip dysplasia can be mild (without symptoms), slightly disabling or severe (causing crippling lameness and arthritis). It is impossible to predict how the condition will progress. There is no cure for hip dysplasia. Prevention through conscientious breeding is the key. Therapy is designed to ease the symptoms and provide your dog a more active and comfortable life. Treatment may consist of:

1) Medication for stiffness and pain.
2) Weight control to reduce the load applied to the painful joint.
3) Physiotherapy, such as swimming or passive joint motion, to reduce the stiffness and maintain muscle integrity.
4) Surgery to provide an improved quality of life.

X-rays can identify abnormal dogs, but may not identify all dogs carrying the disease. Breedings resulting in dysplastic offspring should not be repeated with that pairing.

Hypothyroidism

Hypothyroidism is a hormonal disorder caused by underactive thyroid glands. It is a fairly common disorder of people and pets. Thyroid hormone is essential for the smooth working of the body. If your dog's thyroid level is low, it may lead to fertility problems. The immune system doesn't work as well, so the dog is more prone to infections. Weight gain, poor hair coat, dry skin and increased itching can also be signs of an underactive thyroid gland. The disorder can be confirmed by a blood test. Once the condition is diagnosed, your dog will be (in almost all cases) on thyroid supplementation for the rest of his life. Most commonly, twice-daily supplementation with pills will keep your dog's thyroid at optimum levels. Periodic blood tests are needed to make sure the pills are working at an ideal level. It is not uncommon for your dog to need some adjustments throughout his life.

Immune Disorders (Primary)

A primary immunodeficiency disorder is a diminished ability to mount an immune response, and this is hereditary. All systems of the body are capable of being affected. Symptoms depend on which part of the immune system is defective, and can range from chronic respiratory problems and skin infections to life-threatening conditions. Failure to thrive can be a sign of a primary immunodeficiency disease. Clinical signs may start to appear as maternal antibody levels decrease. There is no cure for primary immunodeficiency disease, and the dog will have an increased chance of infection. It is also possible that more than one littermate may be affected. Antibiotics are used to control infections. Affected animals should not be used in breeding programs.

Osteochondrosis/Osteochondrosis Dissecans

Osteochondrosis (OC) involves the growing cartilage, and leads to its excessive retention. In osteochondrosis dissecans (OCD), a cartilage flap occurs secondary to a fissure that has occurred in this thickened cartilage. The most common joints to be affected with OC are the shoulder, elbow, stifle and hock. Bilateral disease is common. It is seen in large, rapidly growing dogs. OC is a polygenetic disease and its expression is determined by an interaction of genetic and environmental factors. Age of onset can be as young as four months. The most prominent finding is an onset of lameness, sudden or insidious, in one or more limbs that can be slight, moderate or severe, and that becomes worse with exercise. X-rays can help diagnose the condition.

OC is not a treatable condition and may progress to OCD. Surgery is usually required to treat OCD. Restricted weight gain and growth in young puppies may reduce the incidence. Anti-inflammatory drugs can be used to relieve the pain.

Breeding of affected animals should be discouraged. Breedings that result in affected offspring should not be repeated with the same sire and dam.

Panosteitis

Panosteitis is a self-limiting condition found in young, medium- to large-breed dogs that are growing rapidly. The cause of the condition is unknown, and there is no proven genetic transmission. It is most often seen in dogs five to 18 months of age, and males are more commonly affected by a 4:1 ratio. Affected dogs are usually presented because of an acute onset or partial weight-bearing lameness. The puppy may lose her appetite and appear depressed. Other diseases, such as OCD, hip dysplasia and hypertrophic osteodystrophy, need to be ruled out before a diagnosis of panosteitis can be made. Once a diagnosis is made, exercise restriction and aspirin can be used to relieve the pain. The pain may appear to leave one limb only to show up in a different leg — hence the name "shifting leg lameness." The puppy may be intermittently lame for six to 18 months. Usually clinical signs will resolve by the time the dog reaches 18 to 20 months of age. Slowing down the puppy's growth by feeding lower-calorie and lower-protein diets may help decrease the incidence of panosteitis.

Vaginal Hyperplasia

Vaginal hyperplasia (vaginal edema) occurs during estrus, most likely an excessive response to normal estrogen stimulation. The incidence in some breeds or lines may indicate that there is an inherited predisposition for the problem. An owner will notice tissue protruding from the vulva as the bitch is progressing through her season. Spaying is the only way to permanently prevent recurrence. If you want to breed a bitch with hyperplasia, artificial insemination is necessary. The owner needs to keep the protruding vaginal tissue non-traumatized. This involves keeping the area clean and lubricated. An Elizabethan collar or a diaper may be needed to keep the bitch from causing any self-mutilation. As the dog goes out of season and the estrogen levels drop, the vaginal tissue will shrink and disappear back into the vulva. Surgical removal of the hyperplastic tissue during the season is often possible and may prevent recurrence.

Photo Courtesy Michele McGovern

Chapter 9

Showing Your Bullmastiff

Show training starts when the puppy is very young. All training of young puppies should be done with positive reinforcement, as little correction as possible, and in very short sessions.

Once the puppy is settled in her new surroundings, which generally takes several days, training can begin. A few minutes each day, no more than five, should be set aside for her first lessons. If you have a small, stable table (at least two feet by three feet), place a rubber door mat on it and set the puppy squarely on her feet in a balanced position and see if you can make her stand absolutely still for 10 seconds (not as easy as it seems). If the puppy stands still for even five seconds, give her lots of praise and repeat the stand just one more time.

Never let the puppy get bored. If the puppy resists, try to anticipate her moving and release her from her stand just before she moves. That way, the puppy thinks moving was her idea.

Start leash-training the puppy at the same time. Just a few minutes of work is all that is advisable. Some puppies fight as if you were trying to kill them. Others just walk off on the leash, following as if it were an old habit. Use a leather or flat nylon lead. Do not use a chain lead if you value your hands. You may use a buckle collar or a nylon or metal slip collar (choke chain). A choke chain sounds terrible, but it is not. It is an excellent training tool and also the type of collar the dog will be shown on. It only creates pressure when you want to apply it, and releases as soon as pressure is removed. A buckle collar creates essentially the same pressure all the time and is easier for the pup to slip out of. *Never leave a choke chain on a dog when you are not working with him or supervising him closely.*

A good way to convince a puppy to lead is to take a dog biscuit or piece of cooked chicken or liver and hold it just in front of the puppy, exerting a little pressure on the lead. Hold the treat in your left hand with the lead after the puppy gets used to following it. You should not have to keep the lead tight that way and the puppy will travel with his head high, looking at the treat. Soon you will use the treat (or bait) only

occasionally, then not at all for leading, but just as a treat after training sessions. Some trainers don't like to use bait in training, but Bullmastiffs *love* food, and sensible use of treats or bait smooths the path of learning. The key to having a successful training session is to make it enjoyable.

Once the puppy is leading well — that means not lagging nor pulling ahead — you can start practicing the patterns that are required in the ring. If you and the dog become used to these patterns, it doesn't matter which one the judge asks for; you will be ready. Changing patterns while leading the puppy helps keep the session interesting, as the same pattern all the time may bore Bullmastiff puppies. They are always trying to convince their owners that they know a better way to do something. Changing patterns will keep your pup guessing a bit. It would be helpful to attend a show or match prior to the start of this training to observe the different patterns that judges direct exhibitors to use when showing. Talk to several exhibitors who seem particularly competent in working their dogs (after they come out of the ring) and ask how they trained their pups.

The judge will certainly ask the class to go around the ring in a circle as a group. He may also ask you to take the dog in a circle individually. One of the most common patterns for individual work in a class is straight out and back, either to the far corner or just the opposite side of the ring. Practice moving in a straight line with your puppy. Get it used to the pattern so it does not require a tight lead to move where you want it to go.

Another pattern is the triangle. This is generally straight across the ring, a left turn to the corner diagonally opposite from where you started and back to the judge on the diagonal path across the ring. It may also be diagonally across the ring from the judge to the corner, a left turn to the next corner, and a left turn along the side of the ring back to the judge. The judge will tell you exactly where he wants you to move the dog, so it sometimes helps to have someone direct you in training as if he were the judge.

Another less used, but sometimes required pattern is an "L." That is straight across the ring from the judge, a left turn down the side of the ring, an about-face back to the first corner and a right turn back to the judge. This can be a bit tricky. It is not everyone's favorite, since the return trip puts the handler between the dog and the judge, unless the dog is switched to the handler's right side from the about-face and then switched back to the normal left-side position at the right turn for the return to the judge. Most people just leave the dog on the left.

You are far more likely to be asked for a straight out and back and then a circle around the ring, or a triangle and a circle around the ring than you will be asked to do an "L." But it never hurts to be prepared. You are preparing the puppy to show, and showing to her best advantage is the name of the game.

After the puppy is large enough so you don't have to crawl on the ground to stand her squarely (stack her), you can eliminate the table, since that is not used in the show ring for large dogs. While you still have the puppy on the table, after she has learned to stand still for increasing amounts of time, teach the puppy to "stack." Stand the puppy squarely, place her front feet directly under the points of the shoulders, spaced just wide enough to give a squared look to the front. Do not spread the legs far apart to make the dog look wider; she won't — she will look spraddle-legged. Don't put the feet together too closely under the body. That ruins the balanced look and can turn the elbows in and the feet out. Set the rear legs just a very little wider than the body and just very slightly back of it. The leg from the point of the hock to the back of the rear foot should make a perpendicular line to the ground, neither slanting forward or back. If your dog is a little higher in the rear than at the shoulder, which is often the case with growing pups, you can make it appear more level by moving the hind legs back slightly

more than usual. An exaggerated stretching of the rear throws the dog's appearance out of balance.

While you are setting the dog's legs, do not forget to keep a good grip on the collar. Before you set the legs, set the collar where you want it on the dog's neck for maximum control. The best place for the collar during the time the dog is stacked is snugly right behind the ears. When the collar is placed that high on the neck, it tends to gather a fold of skin in front of it under the dog's chin. Be sure you slip the loose skin on the throat behind the collar as you tighten it. That gives a pretty, clean outline of the lead and neck area for the judge. It also gives you maximum control of the dog.

Part of a Bullmastiff's show training involves learning to have his bite, or teeth, checked by a judge. *Photo: Mary Bloom.*

From the beginning of training, teach your dog to submit to having his mouth opened and his teeth looked at. This is very important. A dog that works well but refuses to allow a judge to examine his mouth is not going to be considered for a winning placement.

If you are going to carry bait in the ring, be prepared to carry a clean, small washcloth or paper towel to clean the dog's lips of any drool. Judges hate getting slimed every time they touch a dog's mouth. It's a good idea to carry the cloth, with or without bait. On a warm day, the dog may drool anyway. Carry a cloth during training sessions to get your puppy used to having his mouth wiped.

Many areas have all-breed kennel clubs that hold show-handling classes. If you are lucky enough to be in such an area, take advantage of these classes once you and the puppy have mastered the very basics of standing and leading. If you are not able to do this, get a good book on training.

Remember, you can have your dog thoroughly used to stacking and moving in five to 10 minutes a day, four or five days a week. Make the lessons fun, and give lots of praise. Make the entire training process as positive as possible. At the end of each training session, you can add a few minutes of just plain playtime, but only at the end, after the serious work has been done. Keep practice sessions short, and you will find your dog loving every minute of it.

The Real Thing

Once you and your dog are ready to go to shows, being prepared and knowing how to make the outing comfortable and less stressful is important.

You must enter AKC-licensed shows a full 18 days before the show; in other words, that is the latest date the entries can be received by the show superintendent. Ask your dog's breeder how to contact the show superintendents in your area to be placed on their mailing list. If there is a show nearby, you can go to the superintendent's desk, pick up entry forms (premium lists) for the most recent upcoming shows, and ask to be put on the mailing list. If you need help filling out the entry for the first time, talk to your dog's breeder or a friend who shows, or call the superintendent's office. Once you have completed the entry form for a show, mailed it in or entered electronically, and received your judging schedule in the mail, your work is just beginning.

One or two days before the show, bathe your dog. Never take a dirty dog into the ring. If the weather is too cold to bathe the dog outside and you don't want to put him in the tub or shower, try using a dry shampoo. Brush the dog thoroughly, then apply the dry shampoo. Dry shampoos for dogs can be either foamy or in solution. Work the dry shampoo into the coat well and then rub the dog down thoroughly with a heavy towel.

Trim your dog's nails. (You should be doing this regularly.) Make sure his ears are clean. Most people trim the dog's whiskers. This is all right if you wish to do so, but not absolutely necessary. In fact, the whiskers are the exterior receptors of two large nerve trunks, one on each side of the dog's face. They evidently serve an important purpose. Being shown without having the whiskers trimmed should not prevent the dog from being properly considered by the judge.

You will need either a nylon or metal slip collar (choke chain); either should be as fine as possible and still capable of holding the dog securely. Do not use a coarse, heavy chain for showing. You will need a two- or three-foot-long thin leather show lead (about 1/4 inch thick). It is wise to keep your dog on a heavier walking lead when not in the ring.

The day before the show, prepare a small case with items you may need. Pack a brush, some paper towels, several small towels or washcloths, some Vaseline or baby oil, baby wipes (they come in small packets as well as large), an extra collar, show lead, and any dry treats you want to take along. If it is hot on the day of the show, or there is any chance of it being hot, take a small insulated chest full of ice cubes, a wet towel packed in a plastic bag to retain its moisture, a small spray bottle full of cold water to mist the dog if needed, and cooked or perishable bait for the dog.

Take a folding chair for you and a rug or blanket for your dog to lie on. A folding wire crate is the best way to assure your dog is comfortable and safe if you have to stay for any length of time. The availability and price of food at the shows are not always the same, so bring something to drink and eat in a small cooler if you plan to spend more than an hour or so at the show. That way you will have what you like available.

When dressing to show your dog, dress well but simply and neatly. Avoid dangling jewelry that can interfere with handling your dog, or even upset the animal. Try to wear something with pockets. It gives you a place to put the bait and a washcloth or paper towels. If you are going to use bait in the ring to get your dog's attention, the cloth is a necessity. As I said earlier, the judge is not going to be happy getting a handful of slobber when examining the dog's mouth.

Allow yourself plenty of time to get to the show. It is advisable to arrive one hour before and certainly no less than a half-hour before your scheduled judging time. Parking may be difficult. If you allow enough time for traffic problems on the road and parking problems at the show, you will probably arrive in plenty of time to give the dog a walk to relax and relieve himself.

Then you can put the finishing touches on the dog's grooming with a final brushing, and shining up his coat and face by rubbing a *little* Vaseline or baby oil into your hands and then lightly applying it to the dog. Then give the dog a good wiping down with a clean towel. Do not use excessive oil or coat products on the dog. Use just enough to highlight the good grooming job you've already done.

When in the ring, be attentive to what the judge says. If you do not understand, ask. That is better than doing the wrong pattern or standing in the wrong place. When stacking your dog, try to keep about two feet distance between your dog and the ones in front and behind her. This gives the judge space to see your dog's front and rear clearly and to move around her. It gives you more room to work with your dog. It also is just polite and wise not to crowd another animal in a stressful situation.

If you find you simply don't enjoy being in the ring but want your dog to be shown, there are professional handlers available. It is best to make arrangements for a handler well before the date of the show. Discuss the cost, and watch how the person relates to your dog. Try to find someone who genuinely likes your dog. The dog will be happier and show better. It can be very educational standing outside the ring and watching your own dog work. You can certainly see more of what is going on than when you are on the end of the lead.

If there are fun matches in your area, it is an excellent idea to show a puppy several times at matches before going to a licensed show. The atmosphere is much more relaxed than at licensed shows. You and the puppy will not feel so much pressure to be perfect. No championship points are available at matches. Use the opportunity to practice showing and get the puppy used to performing with other dogs and distractions that she would normally not have at home.

You can start showing a dog in AKC-licensed shows at six months old. (Four- to six-moth competitions are sometimes available, but points are not offered toward a championship.) To get those points, a puppy will have to compete against and defeat adult dogs in the Winners class. Very few puppies are capable of doing this. It is best to start a puppy slowly, increasing the number of shows you enter as the dog matures.

Showing definitely has its ups and downs. If your dog is mature, well balanced, of good type and well presented, she will do her share of winning.

Photo: Courtesy Mona Lindau

Chapter 10

Obedience Training

Obedience training is very advisable for any large-breed dog. For the strong-willed, large dog in an average family setting, it is almost mandatory. As I've said before, Bullmastiffs have a mind of their own. They will try to dominate a situation when given the opportunity.

Like small children, Bullmastiffs need absolute guidelines. And, like small children, they are much happier when the rules are clean and concise. They feel comfortable knowing exactly what is allowed and what is not.

If you are not going to show the dog in obedience, the perfectly square sit and the immobile stand for inspection are not necessary. What is necessary is that the dog follow your commands quickly and every time they are given. Never give a command to a dog and then just let the matter slide if the dog does not obey. Make the dog do what he was told, praise him, then go on to whatever else you want to do.

Basically a timed obstacle course, agility is a fun and fast-paced sport for Bullmastiffs. *Photo courtesy Mona Lindau*

There are any number of books on obedience training available online, in bookshops and at the bookstalls at dog shows. Before buying one, check to see if the author recommends positive reinforcement or uses a negative approach. The Bullmastiff works much better with positive reinforcement. That is not to say you do not correct a dog. You do, but bullying does not work with the Bullmastiff. The best method of obedience training your dog is to join a local class. This only takes up an hour a week, plus no more than 15 minutes a day on non-class days. One day a week with no work helps the dog relax and keeps him keen to get back to his lessons and your attention.

In finding the right instructor, again look for someone who uses positive reinforcement rather than punishment and force. You want the dog to be happy and obey, not resentful or frightened.

There are some areas that have specific classes for puppies. If yours does not, do not take a Bullmastiff to obedience class until he is six months old. Even then, the puppy is growing so fast his ability to retain what he has learned is not always long term. Even though you may not start a puppy in an obedience class until he is six months old, you still need to start his training from the moment he comes into your possession.

Leash-break your puppy, teach him to come on command, and even to sit. Start these lessons within a few days of bringing the puppy home. Establish your household rules immediately and stick to them. Do not give a command and not follow up. Do not allow a dog to do something one day and then discipline him for the same act the next day. If you are consistent and clear in what you want from the dog, he will respect you and be much easier to train.

Obedience training is not just for the obedience ring at shows. Each exercise in the basic Companion Dog program has a purpose in every-day safe and sane living with your dog. Sitting and downing on command can stop a dog from running after a person or a car, from jumping on people or other animals, or is just a good method of controlling a dog

A well-trained Bullmastiff is a pleasure to own.

The goal of training is to keep your Bullmastiff's attention on you. Keep sessions short and sweet — with plenty of treats.

that is overexcited and racing about. Heeling (walking at your side) ensures a pleasant walk with your dog, rather than having your arm stretched and your shoulder ruined in a constant tug of war with a dog determined to go at his own pace. Standing for inspection teaches the dog to stand still when a veterinarian may need to examine the dog. All obedience exercises can be perfected for the ring, but they are definitely major assets in living happily with a dog.

The goal of obedience training is to have a happy, well-mannered, obedient animal. Make sure you make the training sessions short, interesting and fun. The Bullmastiff is extremely smart. She can get easily bored. If a puppy does an exercise correctly, praise her and go on to the next exercise. If you wish to repeat the correctly completed exercise, do so after you have done another. If you are teaching the sit and the dog responds correctly right away, do a minute of heeling before you try the sit again. Think how bored you would be with five minutes of standing up and sitting down again every few seconds.

Keep the lessons short. Start with only five minutes daily, and gradually work your way up to 15 minutes at the most as you add the new exercises. For the household pet who will not enter the ring, five minutes a day, five days a week is sufficient. Once the dog has learned all the lessons well, five minutes two or three times a week to keep them fresh in the dog's mind is all that is necessary. The dog learning obedience for the show ring will need to continue the previous time schedule.

If you make obedience training fun and interesting, the dog will look at lesson time as her own personal time with you away from all other distractions. This is very important to the dog. Bullmastiffs love special attention.

In recommending obedience training, let me make it clear that training for *you and the dog* is what is being recommended. There are trainers who can train your dog for you, but this does *nothing* for the connection between you and your dog. The trainer already knows all about training. The dog learns his part. But unless you participate in the training, you have not learned how to teach your dog and your dog has not learned it is you he is responsible to. The bond developed between owner and dog in training sessions is important. The time you take for one-on-one activities with your dog establishes your position as pack leader in the dog's mind, and also shows the dog you care enough to spend the time with her.

The tools you will need for basic obedience training are a choke chain, a six-foot leather lead and, most important, patience.

Chapter 11
Breeding Bullmastiffs

The first and one of the most important questions to ask is: *"Should you breed your Bullmastiff?"* The idea can be appealing, all those cute little black-faced bundles of joy, the miracle of birth, the good price Bullmastiffs bring, all your friends who "just have to have a pup from your sweet girl."

Now, let's get real. Is your bitch really breeding quality – an animal with very few flaws and lots of virtues? Is her health good, her temperament positive, and her structure correct? Do you have any idea the amount of work that goes into properly supervising this litter from the initial breeding to the time the pups are ready to leave home? That is, if there are any pups, because there's no guarantee there will be. It takes someone with faith, hope and a stubborn streak a mile wide to seriously embark on a breeding program with Bullmastiffs.

Breeding for the sake of breeding, breeding to make money, breeding because you just love your dog and want more of the same, breeding because raising pups looks like a fun thing to do — all are the worst possible reasons to breed a Bullmastiff.

It may sound idealistic, but the real reasons one should breed Bullmastiffs are to better the breed, to give something back to a breed of dog that has given you so much, to produce an even better dog from a dog that is already high quality.

Is your animal sound of body and mind? Is the stud dog equally sound? Are you capable of dealing with a whelping and the raising of pups? Are you ready and willing to make some hard decisions? Are you willing to carefully screen prospective purchasers and willing to keep the pups until proper homes can be found? Do you know how to tube-feed, if necessary, and how to bottle-feed? To stay home and keep an eye on the pups so they come through the first period of their life safely? Now is the time to think about all this; not at 3 a.m. when your bitch is delivering and having a tough time of it. Are you going to be prepared for the worst so the worst doesn't happen? If you can answer yes to these questions, you can think about going ahead with plans to breed.

Having decided to go forward with plans to breed your Bullmastiff, you should already have made sure she is in excellent health, properly vaccinated, and in good physical condition. The dog you will breed her to should have been thoroughly researched before the final decision was made. Do not breed a dog and bitch with the exact same virtues and faults. In looking for a stud dog, find one that is strong where your bitch is weak, a stud dog that does not have any serious faults of his own. Evaluate the two animals to see if they are compatible. Definitely do not choose a dog simply because it is convenient. If you are going to produce puppies, produce the best you can. To do that, go to the best stud dog for your bitch that you can.

If you are using a stud dog belonging to someone else, do not let the dog and bitch even see each other until you have completed and signed a stud-service contract that is fully agreeable to both parties. No matter how friendly you are with the owner of the stud, the passage of time changes people's recollection of what was said. Having a signed contract saves a great many injured feelings.

Nowadays it is not necessary to ship a bitch to a stud dog who lives far away. Chilled or frozen semen can be shipped to your vet and your bitch can be bred without leaving the neighborhood. Shipping semen is not inexpensive, but it is nowhere near as much as shipping the bitch, and much, much easier on her.

Early in the bitch's heat cycle, it is a good idea to have a vaginal smear done to be sure she has no bacterial infections. If there is any sign of infection, the bitch can be put on an antibiotic that will not interfere with conception or the health of the fetuses.

To do a natural breeding, be sure that either you or the owner of the stud is familiar with breeding procedures. *Never* just turn a bitch out with a dog. While that has worked well over the centuries for mongrels in the streets, one would think that the

well-being of your dog means a little more than to take chances. A first-time breeding bitch especially can become quite upset after a tie is established between the dog and bitch. At this time it is essential that there be someone attending each animal to avoid injury to either. Never allow either dog to behave aggressively toward the other.

Today there are a number of tests that can be done to tell you when your bitch is actually ready to breed. If you have both the dog and bitch, it is sometimes no problem at all to tell when she is actually ready. If you are having semen shipped or you have to travel several hours to do a mating, these tests are a tremendous help in pinpointing the proper breeding time, thereby avoiding a lot of aggravation, unnecessary travel, and frustration for you and the dogs.

"Distinguished professional seeks classy lady for a limited-time liaison ..."

If you are going to use shipped semen, you will have to have your bitch tested several times during the heat period to exactly determine the proper day of breeding so that the semen can be shipped the day before you need it and arrive exactly on time. Fresh extended (chilled) semen lives essentially 48 hours. Frozen semen must be used immediately after thawing.

Because this book is meant to cover the basics for newcomers to the breed, I am not going to go into the details of the breeding process. This information is available in excellent books on breeding and genetics. As far as the scientific theories of breeding, I suggest you get a good book on canine breeding theories. This should be done before you attempt the breeding.

You should understand the value of inbreeding (breeding very closely related dogs), linebreeding (breeding related, but not very closely related dogs), and outcrossing (breeding dogs unrelated for four or five generations). All are valuable breeding tools for particular reasons.

If you are doing a natural breeding, do not allow the dog to exhaust himself in futile attempts. If, even with your assistance, a tie cannot be achieved in 10 minutes, the dogs should be taken away from each other completely and allowed to rest for half an hour before another mating is attempted.

Advise your veterinarian in advance that you are planning a breeding on a certain day so that if you have a problem you have assistance. An artificial insemination can be done or the vet may be able to assist in a natural breeding.

Every breeding should be contemplated with the goal of paving a solid, well-planned road ahead — not just for a breeder's individual breeding program, but for the breed at large.

Photo: Kay Reil

Chapter 12

The Stud Dog and Brood Bitch

Both parents should be Bullmastiffs sound in mind and body. They should be in good health and up to date on their vaccine and worming programs. They should be dogs that compliment each other both to the eye and in their genetic makeup. And they should be bred for the purpose of taking the next step in the journey to bettering the breed.

Prospective parents should be sound in mind and body. *Photo: Jerry Vavra.*

Your dog's pedigree is the road map to what your dog will produce. Learn as much as you can about the dogs in that pedigree. The interesting thing about genetics is that a recessive gene (one that doesn't necessarily show up in looking at your dog) can be carried forward without appearing for generations and generations, until it meets up with another recessive from the dog you breed to and pops up in a litter where it is totally unexpected. If you know there are dogs in your bitch's background that carried or produced this recessive factor, and it is a negative trait, try to be sure the same factor is not lurking behind the stud dog.

The more closely related the ancestors of your dog are, the more likely that dog will reproduce what you see in him. If the dog you are mating yours to is very closely related, you will set what you have even more tightly. The further out you cross, the less likely you will be sure the offspring will reproduce their own traits. Remember, inbreeding and tight line breeding set the factors already there. These breeding protocols do not cause anything to show up that is not already present in the dog's genetic makeup. To dilute a factor you want to get rid of, outcrossing to an animal who is tightly bred and does not carry the fault is a good way to help clear your line of a problem. A breeding should be for a purpose, and to accomplish that purpose you have to do your homework.

The Stud Dog

If you own a dog that you are even slightly considering for use as a stud dog, know how to handle a breeding. You will be taking money or a puppy back for a service that is being rendered. The owner of a bitch has the right to expect you to be competent. The safety of both animals and the success of the breeding process are your responsibility. If you feel unable to handle a breeding yourself, make arrangements with your veterinarian to manage the breeding for you.

Are you prepared to safely board a bitch who may have to travel a distance to be bred? With shipped semen available, this may not be a major factor in breeding animals that live a distance away. However, there may be times the bitch's owner does want a physical mating between the two animals. There are more responsibilities than first come to mind in deciding to put a dog at stud.

There are those who think that natural breedings are the only way to go. If a bitch is having a normal heat cycle and the dog is potent, there are no reasons why an artificial breeding at the correct time should not be as successful as a tie. I've always found that to be the case. An artificial insemination may be necessary if the bitch has a vaginal hyperplasia. This condition is described on page 65. It is ugly to look at and can be a source of infection if it prolapses, but the surgical technique to remove it is simple. It only appears when a bitch is in season, or on rare occasions when she is close to delivering her litter. If one is doing an artificial insemination because the dog simply will not show an interest in a bitch, that changes the situation. The dog could be hypothyroid, and have poor sperm quality and a low libido as a result. Thyroid replacement is available and simple to administer. A healthy dog and bitch with normal hormone readings should be able to reproduce no matter how the mating is accomplished.

A very important lesson for a prospective stud dog is obedience to his master. The dog must allow you to manage the breeding. It is particularly important in a breeding dog that he not be raised having his own way whenever he chooses.

It is a good idea to have a sperm check done a few days to a week before doing a mating if the dog has not been bred successfully in the last few months. A test showing the dog has healthy sperm and lots of it is always a good thing to know. Especially if the bitch does not conceive after being bred.

The Brood Bitch

Once the breeding is accomplished, the real work will start for the owner of the bitch. Some bitches breeze right through a pregnancy, deliver naturally and do everything by the book. Don't count on having one of those.

Remember that just as with the stud dog, the brood bitch must allow human management of the breeding to the extent it is necessary. Spoiling your sweet girl by having her sleep with you at all times is just fine for pets, but disaster for breeding bitches. Wait until you wake up in the middle of the night with afterbirth and the usual guck associated with delivery all over your new quilt. The stuff doesn't wash out, either. Then comes the news that she won't stay in a whelping box with those noisy little demanding creatures. She wants back in with Mom and/or Dad. Since having pups was your idea, you can take care of them. Sooo, establish early on that where you put her is where she sleeps. Get her used to a whelping box weeks before she is due. A bitch who understands she is really a canine will give you far less trouble than one who has been taught she is your child. She will generally be a happy, attentive mother, although there are exceptions to that.

Some bitches have no milk at first and may never have milk come in. In these cases, you will have to feed by bottle or tube. (Your vet can give you a good tube-feeding demonstration before the need arises.) Tube-feeding is fine for the first few days, but after that bottle-feeding works much better until 3½ to 4 weeks, when the puppies start dish-feeding. Some bitches have poor mothering instincts to begin with. You may have to insist on the bitch laying still for the pups to nurse because she doesn't really understand what is going on. This is more likely to occur if this is the bitch's first litter and it was by Caesarian section. Once a bitch has suckled pups, she doesn't forget how.

An attractive female head study.

Don't wait until the last minute to be prepared for all possibilities. Have a clear understanding with your veterinarian that if you feel the delivery is not going properly, your vet will be there to do what needs to be done. Also find out well in advance what the fee will be. Some vets charge $400 and others have managed to ask $1,000 without blushing. If you have to, shop around for a vet who is familiar with breeding procedures and surgical deliveries and is reasonable in his or her charges. Don't get yourself in a position where you have no maneuverability because you waited until the last minute.

If you think you are going to save money by waiting as long as possible in the hopes the bitch will stop having trouble and just go right ahead and deliver, think again. The worst kind of Caesarian is the one done under emergency conditions when the bitch is already exhausted. If you are going to put a monetary value on the procedure, think about delaying and losing several pups because of that. You could have paid for three or four surgeries with the price of the puppies you lost.

Just about to pop: Navigating a successful pregnancy with your Bullmastiff involves lots of preparation, and not a little good luck.

Don't insist on a Caesarian just because you are nervous about the delivery. A natural whelping is still the ideal. However, if common sense tells you your bitch needs help, don't take no for an answer. Have that absolutely settled as soon as you know the bitch is in whelp. Do find another vet if yours will not guarantee availability at that time. Some vets insist that Caesarians are emergency procedures. They may sometimes be emergencies, but that is not always the case. If you know your bitch is having real trouble whelping, do not wait until you risk bitch and pups.

Bullmastiffs can have primary uterine inertia, in which case the bitch will not have any effective labor. A bitch who has delivered several pups but doesn't finish the job because the muscles of the uterus are exhausted has secondary uterine inertia. Sometimes a bitch cannot pass a puppy because it has an abnormal presentation in the birth canal. A bitch's uterus is structured in two long horns leading to one junction at the opening of the birth canal. If two puppies arrive at the same time, the traffic jam can create a problem in delivery. A puppy can also present transversely or backwards (breech presentation). Many pups are born breech, but if it is the first pup in the litter to be born and the head is large, it can present quite a problem for the bitch. There are also rare occasions where the uterus forms a kink around the pup, effectively locking it in so that no number of contractions will deliver it. The continued contractions can even cause the rupture of the uterine wall. *Never* induce stronger contractions by giving oxytocin or pituitrin shots or drops to a bitch having trouble delivering until an X-ray determines there is no such problem. It's a great way to lose the bitch and the litter. There are times when these hormones can be safely used, but it must be with discretion. If a bitch is taking an unusually long time to deliver due to any of these reasons, I prefer taking the pups surgically rather than risking her and the pups with an overlong, exhausting labor. Bullmastiff bitches can separate the puppies' placental attachment to the uterus with no visible contractions. Carefully consider whether to continue a natural delivery or do a Caesarian, taking into account all possibilities.

In nature, the fittest survive. Bitches who can whelp naturally with no trouble at all are the ones who would survive, and so would their pups. However, humans have decided to produce dogs that are built a certain way and look a certain way for certain purposes. Remembering that "It's not nice to fool with Mother Nature," we have to accept that there are sometimes prices to pay for our artistic design endeavors in dog breeding.

If you are too interested to wait until your bitch starts to noticeably enlarge to find out if puppies are on the way, you can have an ultrasound done at 3½ weeks. If you do this, you can also have a blood test done to see that she has the proper hormone level to carry through a pregnancy. Bitches can, especially at about five weeks along, resorb their litters due to a drop in hormone level. Many bitches that were thought to have

false pregnancies after a breeding actually resorbed their litters.

Taking as fact that your brood bitch is in whelp and everything is going along normally, the following procedures should be done. Feed your bitch as you always have through at least the first five weeks. She will probably be ravenously hungry, but that doesn't mean you should turn her into Petunia Pig because she has massive food cravings. You may find you cannot tell if you have a fat bitch or a pregnant one if you start stuffing her little tummy as soon as you breed her. If the bitch is in the good condition she should be in when she was bred, she can do quite nicely the first five weeks without a lot of extra food. When you start adding to her diet, do it gradually and divide the food into several extra meals daily. If she gets very large meals she will not have room to eat large amounts at one time. Toward the end of a pregnancy three or four meals a day will help her make the best use of her food. I do not recommend supplementing a bitch. If you are feeding her good-quality food, it should be sufficient.

A few weeks before the due date, set up her whelping box in a draft-free place out of the heavy household traffic flow and get her used to the whelping box. Set up a heat lamp about five to six feet above the box. (That is, if it isn't mid-summer and the temperature in the house is 90 degrees and up.) When you turn it on, angle it so the heat covers only half the box. The bitch can keep the pups warm when they are against her body. She will be spending a lot of time in it for the few weeks after delivery.

When she is about three days from her first due date, take her temperature rectally. The dog's normal temperature is about 100.5 to 101.5 F. When she is within 24 hours of whelping, her temperature will drop to 99 degrees or even lower, and stay down until the time she is whelping. If the temperature drops and then goes up in a few hours, I usually find the bitch is 48 hours from delivery. Realize that this is the general rule. I've had brood bitches that never dropped their temperature at all and delivered normally.

The bitch will also become very quiet and sleep deeply a day or two before she whelps. She will generally start to pace and/or pant when she starts active labor. If your bitch is anything like mine, that usually occurs at 11 p.m. after a hopelessly busy day. Their timing is amazing!

How many does she have in there? Would you believe 11?

Put together a "birthing kit" several weeks before the due date. It should include the following: small clean towels, sturdy paper towels, scissors, dental floss (for tying off the cords), alcohol (for sterilizing scissors), infant nasal syringe (for clearing nostrils and throat if necessary), a clean box or large plastic dishpan for holding pups while the bitch is delivering, a heating pad (never put the pups directly on the pad), baby bottles and preemie nipples, milk substitute, bottled electrolyte solution, a feeding tube and syringe, a thermometer and baby wipes. Have lots of newspapers and acrylic fleeces, or even blankets, on hand for the whelping box. I personally don't care for large blankets as the pups tend to get buried in them. I put three or four layers of newspaper down and lay a large fleece in the middle of the box.

There are a number of bitch's milk replacers on the market. You can use one of those or either of the following: goat's milk diluted by 20 percent with an oral electrolyte solution for the first two days and with bottled water thereafter. Or, I have found the following formula to be a successful bitch's milk replacer: 1 can evaporated milk, equal amount of bottled water (except for the first two days, when I use an oral electrolyte in equal amount as the milk), 1 egg yolk, 2 tablespoons plain yogurt, 1 tablespoon mayonnaise. Mix this in a blender, strain and store in a covered jar in the refrigerator until needed. Warm to a comfortable heat when tested on your wrist before feeding.

Be sure your whelping box is large enough in either direction for your bitch to lie stretched out on her side full length. Have a pig rail (½ inch x 4 inch x inner measurement of box) around the inner edge of the box. It should be four inches above the floor of the box. A bitch who lies against the side of a whelping box can crush her pups. With a pig rail, the babies can crawl under the rail while the mother lies against it.

Do not have all your friends, children and other family members coming in a constant stream to see your wonderful new puppies. This will agitate the bitch and she is likely to crush puppies trying to cover them up or step on them. There will be plenty of time for the pups to be seen. Let the bitch have peace and quiet. She needs it and deserves it. The fewer the distractions, the better she will settle in to care for her litter.

Check the bitch's breasts daily to be sure she does not develop mastitis (inflammatory infection in the breasts). A puppy sucking from an infected teat can become critically ill. The condition also causes the bitch severe pain, and she may not allow her pups to nurse if mastitis develops. If your bitch does develop mastitis, ask your vet for an antibiotic that is safe for the puppies. You may even have to remove them from her for a few days until the infection clears. You can often milk the infection from the affected teat or teats. You will get a bloody pus discharge. If you milk the bitch's infected teat, do it every hour for several times until you get an actual milk discharge. Use the antibiotic. Milking is not a replacement for antibiotic treatment.

Watch your bitch for vaginal discharge after delivery. Bitches that have had Caesarians very likely may discharge more heavily than bitches who have had natural deliveries. The bitches can pass clots as well as liquid discharge. The discharge can last from just a few days to weeks. The heaviest discharge will come in the first day or two. Be sure there is no pus or other sign of infection. If the bitch has had a Caesarian, she may run a little temperature for a day or two after delivery. A bitch with a natural delivery should not.

Watch out for eclampsia. The production of milk can cause a bitch's blood calcium to drop severely: Although right after a surgical delivery a bitch may shiver for a few hours because of the shock to her system, be sure to watch carefully to make sure that is all it is. If the shivering is from the surgery itself, a heat lamp and a blanket should clear up the problem in short order. Eclampsia shivering can turn to seizures: The bitch can lose consciousness and die if not treated. If you suspect eclampsia, call your vet immediately. The bitch needs calcium. Once she is given a calcium injection, the recovery is almost immediate and amazing.

If the bitch shows aggression toward her pups, either muzzle her and sit with her while they nurse or remove them from her. Occasionally the massive hormone swings associated with giving birth can disorient her, especially if the birth was surgical. Often this tendency passes in a day or two, and the bitch is a loving mother. The vast majority of deliveries you will not face this problem, but you need to be aware it can happen.

The fact that I've described what can go wrong doesn't mean it will. You now know the possibilities and can watch out for them. You now know breeding Bullmastiffs may not be as easy as it seems. The whole process may also go as smooth as silk. A successful breeding of two high-quality Bullmastiffs is worth the effort to know how to proceed and how to do it properly

Chapter 13

The Babies

Anywhere from six hours to even five minutes before the birth of the first pup, your Bullmastiff will start panting. Constant panting is a sign that you can put all your other plans on the back burner. For some reason, the majority of bitches seem to like to start this procedure late at night.

As mentioned in the previous chapter, when the bitch is within 24 hours of delivery, her temperature should drop to 99 degrees Fahrenheit, or very close to it, and hold steady. She will probably be doing a lot of deep sleeping. She may spend several days shredding or rearranging the bedding you so carefully put in the box for her. It is a natural process. You can straighten the box up again, but it is guaranteed she will redo it to her liking.

As whelping time nears, the bitch may circle in the whelping box, she may look at her rear, she can even throw up her latest meal. All this is normal procedure. If she is thirsty, give her small amounts of fluid at a time. The best thing to give her is an oral electrolyte (available in the baby section of your supermarket, the plain not the fruity flavor). This is used to rehydrate and nourish human babies with diarrhea. It gives your bitch much more support than plain water. A cup at a time at half-hour or hour intervals is a reasonable portion. If the bitch drinks heavily she will just throw it up. The bitch may lie down and rise often. She is obviously uncomfortable. She is also trying to place herself in just the right position for delivery.

Be sure you have all your necessities with you. Have your box with soft toweling in the bottom, a heating pad set on medium draped over one inside panel, and a towel covering it to hold the heat in the box. While the bitch is delivering each pup, the others can be safely held in the box in a corner of the whelping box. The bitch can nurse the already arrived pups between deliveries.

While waiting for the puppies to make their appearance, check for any vaginal discharge. Mucous, mucous streaked with a little blood or a clear fluid are normal. If you see a very dark, almost black discharge, or a deep green discharge, call the vet. This means a placenta has separated, and the odds aren't good for that pup. He cannot survive without the oxygen supplied through the cord and placenta. He can also bleed out through the detached placenta. It might be that this is the only pup that has separated, or there could be more. One thing is sure: That pup cannot be allowed to remain very long in the uterus without the possible contamination of the other pups. Decomposition does not take long to start. If you see this type of discharge, and the bitch delivers the pup very shortly after, it is possible that the pup can make it. Sometimes there is only a partial separation, and there is enough oxygen to keep the pup going until he is born. If the bitch does deliver this pup alive, and proceeds normally to deliver another, you may want to allow her to continue. If there is a question in your mind as to the safety of the remaining pups, a decision should be made at this time whether or not to do a surgical delivery.

At the time the puppy is about to make an appearance, the bitch will generally curl her body back toward her vulva, which exerts extra pressure to assist the progress of the pup and puts her in a position to tear open the sac, cut the cord and wash the pup. She will most likely want to eat the afterbirth. Let her. It is highly nutritious and contains material that will help her milk production. If she has more than a half-dozen pups, you don't have to let her eat all the placentas.

If the bitch does not tear the sac, cut the cord and start the pup breathing, that becomes your job. The first step is to tear open the end of the sac around the pup's head. Use a clean towel or paper towel to wipe the face clean and clear the mouth and nostrils. If the pup is not breathing, give him a good brisk rubbing in both directions on his rib cage. Tie the cord with cotton string or ready-made umbilical clips *no closer* than one inch from the body. Cut the cord *outside* that tie, between the tie and the placenta. If the pup is very congested or not breathing, you need to help. Pick up the pup in a dry, clean towel. Lay him on the open palm of your hand on his back with his head securely gripped between your thumb and fingers. Hold the body steady with your other hand: *it is absolutely necessary that the neck be stabilized and not allowed to move separately from the body.* Stand up where you have lots of clear space. Holding the puppy head down, swing the puppy between your legs and up again. Remember to have lots of space. You don't want the pup to be knocked against anything. The centrifugal force will pull fluids out of the respiratory system. Swing the pup several times and then rub him briskly. Most puppies that are congested take only a minute to clear. You may have to work a half-hour to get a tough one really started. You can also lay the pup on your palm as previously described and, completely covering his mouth and nose with your mouth, puff gently into his mouth (remember how tiny his lung capacity is). Puff and then gently squeeze the rib cage or bend the pup's head over his chest toward his tail to expel that air. Do that three or four times and then do the swinging process again. I can't stress enough the necessity of the support of the neck and full spine. Also hang on tight. Swinging a pup that flies out of your hands can be disconcerting for you and definitely bad news for the pup. You can also use a baby nose syringe to pull fluid out of a pup's throat and breathing passages.

If the bitch needs some help passing a puppy, you can carefully take hold of the head and neck, or the rear, if it is presenting that direction, with a clean washcloth or paper towel and pull *slowly* and *gently* downward toward the bitch's feet, not straight out under her tail, *with each contraction*. If you think the bitch is unable to pass the visible pup and she is not having contractions, you can pull *gently* in the same direction. There may be times when the pup is mainly in the vulva but not outside the body and isn't progressing. You can reach in and grasp the head or hips *very carefully* and maneuver the pup out. If he is really stuck, get to the vet. Pulling against very strong resistance can kill the pup.

Most puppies delivered naturally will start breathing on their own. If the bitch tears the sac and cuts the cord she will roughly wash the pup, rolling him around in the box to agitate him while she cleans him. That usually causes the little one to seriously complain,

getting lots of oxygen in the process.

You can tear open and remove the sac and cut and tie the cord and then let the bitch clean up the pup if you feel it is necessary to be involved.

Be absolutely sure you see a placenta for each puppy. The exception to your being able to do that is if the bitch has delivered one when you weren't in the room. If

Contemplating a job well done.

the pup is cleaned up, she probably already ate the afterbirth. Retained placentas can cause severe infection. Therefore it is a good idea when you think the last pup has been born to go to the vet as soon as possible to get a clean-out (oxytocin or pituitrin) shot for the bitch. The vet can also palpate her abdomen and check her over to be sure she is all right.

If you have not done so with each birth, have the vet check each puppy for any visible congenital or hereditary defects. Several very important problems to check for are harelip, which is very obvious, as the upper lip is split. A cleft palate (a harelip can be part of this problem if the cleft is placed forward enough) is an opening on the roof of the mouth (palate) that can be a tiny hole or a massive trench. It can also be in the

THE BABIES

soft palate at the rear of the mouth, almost invisible without careful inspection. These puppies should be put to sleep since they are extremely difficult to feed and require expensive surgery that may not have completely successful results. A harelip prevents a pup from successfully nursing, but if it is not combined with a cleft palate can be surgically corrected. These pups should be neutered or spayed.

An incomplete abdominal closure (basically around the umbilical cord) may appear like a larger form of an umbilical hernia, but it is not. The area around the cord is the last place on the abdomen for the muscle tissue to grow together. This gives the cord room to expand while the pup is in the uterus. Sometimes this closure does not occur. Umbilical hernias are usually due to excessive pulling of the cord during the birth process or as the cord is being severed. The muscle tissue under the immediate area is fully formed and the opening in the muscle feels like a slit. In the case of an incomplete abdominal closure, the muscle tissue thins from the normal area to nonexistent at the center of the opening. Sometimes pups are born with

Newborn puppy.

a clear membrane over the whole abdomen – definitely candidates for euthanasia. Some are born with an opening the size of a nickel to a quarter. This defect can be congenital and it can be hereditary. Certain dogs have consistently produced a pup or more in each litter with this defect. It can come from either parent. If the opening is small enough to be corrected, the pup should be sold as a pet with an ironclad spay/neuter agreement.

An extremely serious defect is an incomplete anal opening. There is a seal over the rectal opening. It is seldom a successful process to try to surgically correct this, as there are usually other incomplete connections further up the intestinal tract. The kindest thing to do is to euthanize these pups. This is an uncommon occurrence, but not a rarity. Check puppies right after birth to be sure they can have a bowel movement.

"Water puppies" are very obvious. They look like stuffed toys, and their tissues are engorged with fluid. There is no use in trying to save these pups. Heart anomalies are also a possibility. Your vet can check pups for this. These are the most common defects you will see, if you see any. Most litters are quite within the norm.

Be sure each puppy defecates and urinates. The first few bowel movements consist of a material called meconium. Without a doubt it's the stickiest stuff outside of superglue. If the bitch is caring for the pups she will stimulate them with licking their bellies and rears and rolling them around until they eliminate. If you are stuck with the job, use baby wipes, moistened cotton balls or facial tissue. Stroke the rectum over and over in one direction to stimulate elimination. With male pups do the same over the sheath. If you hold them and do the rectum they will wet all over you, so it's easier to stimulate their urination first. Some puppies need stimulation for a week before they eliminate on their own. Others get started on their own within a day. Doing the stimulation on hand-raised pups keeps them much cleaner than allowing them to eliminate all over themselves. Any irritation in the rectal or abdominal area can be soothed with either A&D Ointment or Desitin. Do not allow urine or feces to remain on the pup's skin.

It is extremely important that the pups be kept warm at all times. Puppies do not develop an internal thermostat until they are at least 10 days old. They have no shiver reflex to help warm them. A chilled puppy is in serious danger. It is not necessary to fry the pups, the bitch and everyone else in the house by keep the room at a high temperature. Keeping a heat lamp focused on the side of the box the bitch is not laying in keeps the area at a safe heat level for the pups. The room should be warm, but it does not have to be in the 90-degree range. If you get the area around the box too warm, the bitch will overheat and not want to stay with the pups.

You can tell when pups are too warm or too cold: If the pups are too warm, they will spread out far from each other in the box. Their tongues will appear very red. They can be very agitated or limp like little dishrags. If the pups are too cold, they will climb into a tight pile and whimper a great deal. In short order they can become very quiet and depressed.

A really chilled pup should never be fed formula or allowed to nurse until he has been properly warmed. This is done by wrapping him in a heated towel or placing him next to a heating pad. Placing a weak puppy directly on a heating pad can cause severe burns and even death, as he cannot move to avoid overheating. You can also wrap a pup in a small towel and place him under your shirt or even under your armpit. The warming must be done by radiant heating, not by ingestion of warm fluids. When the pup appears to have regained normal body temperature for his age, then he can be fed. A neonatal puppy does not have as high a body temperature as an adult.

Just because new pups climb all over each other or wander off separately in the box does not mean they are either chilled or overheated. They can do both without being in trouble. The signs of chilling or overheating are evidenced by extreme examples of piling or dispersing.

It is very important that the puppies nurse from their mother to get colostrum. Only the fluid in the first 24 hours after birth contains colostrum. Colostrum carries the immune factors the puppies need. If the bitch is not interested in feeding her puppies, you should try to milk her and see that each pup gets a cc or two of colostrum.

Some puppies have trouble managing a baby-bottle nipple at first if you need to supplement or completely feed them. Some are too weak to suckle. In this case, a knowledge of tube-feeding is a benefit beyond telling. Puppies do not have a gag reflex in the first few days of life, so they don't fight the insertion of the tube. Your vet can give you instructions on tube-feeding in just a few minutes. You can also get tube feeding instructions from the internet; search on Youtube.com or other informational sites.

If you are going to tube-feed, do it often and in small amounts. *Never* fill a puppy's stomach until it feels solid when palpated through the abdominal wall. Five to 10 ccs are plenty at one time in the first few days of a puppy's life. For the first week, feedings should be every two hours if the pup is tube-fed. Keep several fingers over the area where you can feel the stomach (not the abdomen) expanding as you feed. Stop before the stomach completely fills to a hard consistency. You will make the pup very sick by overfeeding. The amount you feed is determined by how much each pup can take without the stomach feeling hard.

If you bottle-feed, you may have to slightly pinch the pup's lips around the nipple to get a good suction started. Be sure the milk is at a comfortably warm temperature. Tighten the cap as much as you can to reduce the flow of milk. Stroking the puppy's throat while he is starting to suck gets his swallowing reflex working better. If the milk is flowing too fast, the puppy may blow it out his nose. Do not panic. Tip the pup's head down, clear his mouth and nose by wiping it off or even swinging him as you would have done to clear his passages at birth (supporting his neck at all times). Sometimes this happens because the pup is in too big a hurry, and sometimes because he just can't coordinate sucking and swallowing. If the pup can't get the hang of it in a couple of tries, go to tube-feeding. Sometimes it takes several days for the pup to be coordinated enough to use a baby bottle.

If your bitch is feeding the pups but needs to have the pups supplemented because she hasn't got quite enough milk, you may find the little "hardhead" who isn't going to suck on anything but mom; he is a candidate for tubing if assistance is a necessity. Then there are those pups that won't take a bottle unless you let them find the nipple themselves. If you put it in their mouth, they spit it out. If you put it near their nose, they find it and suck.

Just because a bitch lets puppies nurse does not mean she has enough milk. Keep an eye on the babies to make sure they are not dehydrating for lack of fluid. Signs of dehydration can be a coat that is dull and starey (dry, upright hairs rather than soft hairs lying close against the body); skinny bodies with ribs showing, and fussy, crying pups. Pick up the skin on the back of a pup's neck and let it drop. It should fall right back into place. If it stays pinched together and upright, that pup is severely dehydrated. This is where oral electrolytes are invaluable. Be sure the formula for the next 24 hours is made with that instead of water.

If the bitch is feeding the litter herself, it is a good idea to watch out for the piglets in the litter overriding the smaller pups. Be sure all get their fair share of nursing. The dominant pups in a litter can finish off the supply in their nipple and just move right down the line, shoving other pups away and drinking their share, too. If you have a smaller or weaker pup, be sure to sit with him periodically to see he gets his share or give him a supplemental feeding.

New puppies should show signs of movement in their sleep. It is called activated sleep. They seem to twitch at odd times for no reason. This is a healthy sign.

Be careful when the bitch is leaving or entering the box or changing her position. Some bitches are meticulously careful about their pups. Others just flop down wherever the mood takes them, whether a pup is lying there or not. It is best to supervise the mother's comings and goings for several weeks.

A pile of newborn puppies.

After the whole litter has arrived, weigh each newborn. It is not necessary but it makes for an interesting reference. The one thing you need to be sure of is that all the pups are gaining daily. The very first 24 hours some may lose an ounce or part of an ounce. That can be from the fact that they were floating in a fluid and now have passed a lot of that out of their tissues. By day two, all the pups should be making steady weight gains. Each pup will not gain the same as the others, as they didn't all start out at exactly the same weight. You can tell by looking at a puppy if he is thriving. He has a plump but not swollen, sleek look. He shows activated sleep. He is a hearty nurser.

THE BABIES

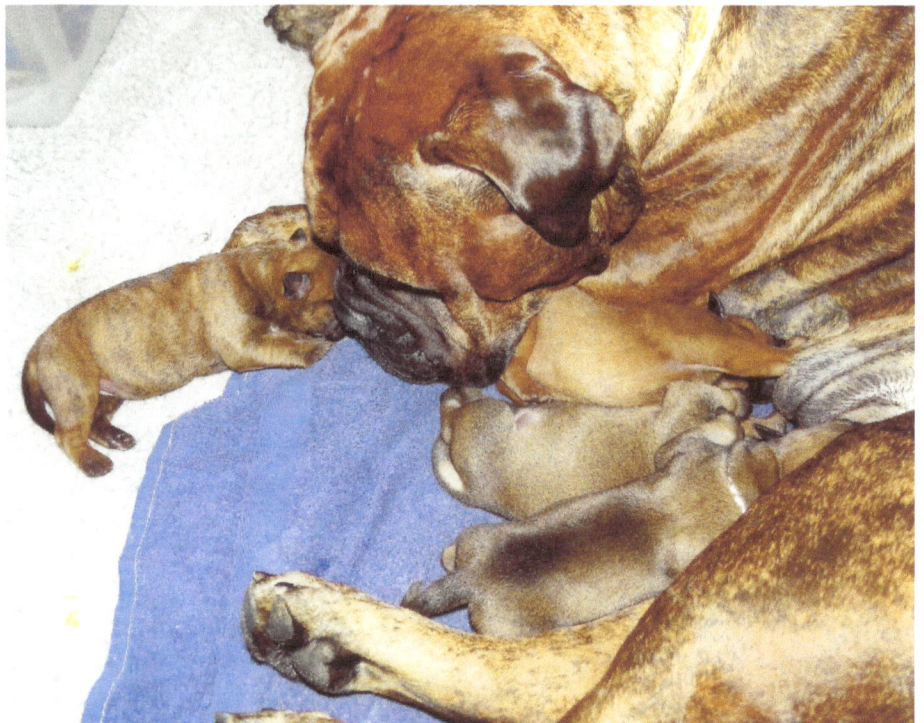

Keep track of puppy weights to ensure all are gaining steadily.

Your puppies' temperaments were born with them. You can tell by careful observation who are going to be the dominant dogs almost immediately. You can also tell who are going to be the kind to suffer in silence and who are going to be the noisy complainers. They start right away. You can learn a great deal by simply sitting beside the whelping box and observing the puppies' behaviors.

There are two more undesirable genetic characteristics that are immediately or very soon obvious in a litter. Most pups are born with pink noses, which color in a matter of days. These pups will have black masks, or they may actually have no masks. Either way, that is essentially normal pigmentation. The problem is when the nose is bright pink and the mask is red or blue. These pups are Dudleys. The term comes from the name of Lord Dudley, who raised white Bulldogs. Dudleys are a dilute color factor. As adults, they will always have yellow eyes. At first, the eyes will be a beautiful baby blue. This you can't tell until the pup is 10 days to two weeks old, when the eyes open. Almost all pups' eyes have a very dark blue shade when they first open, but never this bright baby blue. These puppies are strictly pet stock, should be altered, and should never be shown or bred. They are exactly the same as any normally pigmented pup except for their pigmentation. Puppies like this are produced by breeding two animals carrying the recessive genetic factor for Dudleyism. It is never an accident of nature. This is programmed into them, just as the normal inherited pigmentation is programmed into other pups. To be a Dudley the pup must have the blue or red mask; blue, pink or cherry nose leather, and yellow eyes. Dogs can have very light eyes without being Dudleys. A major step in eliminating this problem is to never breed a known carrier to a known carrier.

The second undesirable genetic characteristic is long hair. These are absolutely adorable pups. Their coats are not just longer representations of the normal coat: The coat is of the same type as a Golden Retriever, spaniel or setter. The pups are usually born coal black, or with a heavy coal black overlay. They will eventually turn red, fawn or brindle. At anywhere from three to 10 days their ears and lips will show fringe along the edges. The coats can be straight or develop a beautiful wave. They are normal Bullmastiffs in every respect except in the type of coat they carry. These too are dogs to be altered and never shown or bred.

If you come up with either of these characteristics your litter, do some research to trace the genetic influence. There will be some people willing to help. You need not feel guilty about producing these pups. It is something that can lay hidden for generations. It is important to find out where the genetic links are to avoid doing this again, just as with any undesirable genetic trait. The reason one would not want to keep reproducing these pups is that they are unshowable and unbreedable by any ethical person. Why not breed for the ultimate number of top-quality pups? In other words, if you are going to breed, do it for the highest benefit to the breed.

If you have gotten through the first week with your litter, you are probably waiting impatiently for their eyes to open. This occurs from 10 to 14 days after birth. If prior to the time the eyes open you see swelling under the lids (frog eyes) or pus seeping out of a tiny opening at the edge of the lid, carefully open the lid. It isn't easy, so if you don't feel comfortable doing it, get to the vet *immediately*. An hour can be the difference between a puppy with perfect vision and a blind dog. What causes this condition is a systemic infection. The pup must be put on antibiotics immediately and have his affected eye or eyes treated with antibiotic ophthalmic ointment at multiple times daily. If the lids are open in time to avoid damage from the extreme pressure and infection, the pup should be perfectly normal. This is not a common occurrence, but it can happen, and you should just keep a careful watch until the eyes do open.

If it does happen, the pup must go to the vet immediately. Allowing the eyelids to remain sealed with this condition will destroy the eye. The vet can gently peel the lids apart and insert antibiotic ointment, and show you how to do this a few times a day for several days.

When the pups' eyes open, do not expose them to really bright light for the first week. They do not see clearly anyway. They find their way around by smell. If they look at you in a somewhat strange manner, it is just that they see a fuzzy form.

After two and a half to three weeks, the puppies' ears open. Up to this time, they are sealed. Mother Nature is very clever in this. A puppy that cannot see nor hear is not startled or upset by any unusual activity around him. As long as he can smell and reach his mother, he is contented to eat, sleep, eliminate and grow without distraction.

The pups may find their voices before they hear. It is funny to see and hear a pup sitting in the box barking at his littermates, who are totally ignoring him because they can't hear him. Even funnier is to see the reaction of a pup the first time he hears himself bark.

This is a wonderful age. The pups are learning so much so quickly. They make their first drunken attempts to walk, they begin to take notice of the fuzzy world around them. They recognize you mostly by your scent and stumble across the box to greet you.

Shortly after two weeks of age, the tips of the puppies' first teeth break through the gums. By three and a half weeks, the enthusiastic nursers are their mother's worst nightmare. This is a good time to give her some short periods completely away from the pups (half an hour) and introduce them to dish feeding. I like to mix a bit of human baby rice cereal with some ground and soaked *adult* kibble and canned milk, yogurt and warm water. I make it the consistency of a very thick soup. The circular puppy feeding pans with a raised core are very helpful in keeping the greedy ones from shoving all the way across the pan. In fact, I generally introduce each puppy to dish feeding by holding him and a custard cup in each hand, away from the others, and on a lot of newspaper. I keep a number of paper towels handy for face wiping. After a couple of sessions like this, they get the idea of lapping from a bowl without drowning, and I can try an "all around the big pan" feeding. Unless you can remain very calm, don't watch the first communal meal. It's a mess! As the pups get better at dish feeding, you can thicken the mixture. Start leaving out the baby cereal. Then start soaking whole kibble and mashing it up with the other ingredients. Gradually make the mix drier and less mashed, so that by seven weeks the pups are eating well-moistened kibble with a little canned food and warm water.

The best time to start weaning seems to be around 4 to 4 ½ weeks of age. Let the mother stay with the pups at night until 4½ to 5 weeks. Take the bitch away from the pups a good half-hour before feeding them. Feed them a good meal before she is allowed in with them. They will suckle a little bit, not their usual amount. They start on six meals a day, gradually working their way down to three meals daily by 7½ weeks.

Dinnertime! A "flying-saucer"-style feeding pan is handy for large litters.

When the bitch is fully removed from the pups, place a fairly shallow dish of water in their box. They will need more fluid than the solid food provides.

To assist the bitch in drying up her milk supply, give her only a very small amount of water the first day she is away from the pups completely. Give her only half her normal food ration. The next day, give her enough water to ease her thirst but not free access. Give her about 2/3 of her normal meal. On the third day, feed her the same amount of food she normally ate before pregnancy. Let her drink what she wants within reason. Check her breasts to be sure she does not have any inflammation. She will probably be heavily engorged for the better part of a week, so keep a careful watch.

If the weather is good, the puppies can go outside for a short period of time once or twice a day for two or three days. Weather permitting, they can then spend all the warm part of the day outdoors. The amount of outdoor time is dependent on the season and the area of the country in which you live. If it is summer, the pups can sleep in outdoor dog housing by the time they are 6 to 6 ½ weeks old. Again, common sense should dictate the amount of time the puppies spend outside.

You will find that the more time they do spend outside, the better they seem to grow. Their activity tends to help them make better use of their food.

My own vaccine and worming schedule is as follows: Round and tapeworm treatments (we are in a flea area) at 4 to 5 weeks of age. Re-treat at 7 ½ weeks if any pups pass worms on the first treatment. Puppies living together constantly reinfest each other. New owners are asked to have their puppies' stools checked by the vet at three months to see that the puppies are clear of worms. At six weeks I give DHLPP (distemper, canine hepatitis, leptospirosis, parainfluenza, parvo). Killed vaccine wherever possible, especially the parvo vaccine. I also give bordetella (Intra-Trac II) kennel cough nose drops. I prefer the nose drops to the injectable vaccine. It goes directly to the respiratory system. At 11 weeks I repeat the DHLPP (again, killed vaccine) and give the first coronavirus vaccine (killed vaccine). At four months the pups receive DHLPP, corona (killed vaccine) and their rabies vaccine. In some areas Lyme disease vaccines are necessary. If the pups have left home, the schedule is given to the new owners. The boosters for all these vaccines are given at 16 months. Thereafter boosters should be no closer than yearly and most rabies vaccines given after the first year are of three-year duration. Some veterinarians feel that puppies should be vaccinated every two weeks from six weeks until four months. I am personally against that, as I believe it seriously overstresses the immune system. My schedule has worked very well for me. I am sure other breeders have their own regimen.

Puppies should be handled, played with and introduced to new sights and sounds as much as their confinement to the property allows. It is not wise to take the pups off the property with their immunity not at full strength.

When you have puppies, you seem to be suddenly popular, and everyone wants to visit and see the babies. It is not a good idea to stress the bitch with a lot of visitors or even anyone she doesn't know when she is nursing her pups. Everyone who comes to the whelping box from outside is a carrier of germs, bacteria and viruses that the adult dogs may be immune to, but not the pups. It is very tempting to show off your lovely pups, but the possibility of turning them into really sick babies increases with each person who visits them. It is best to wait until you have the first vaccines in the pups before inviting friends and prospective buyers to your house to visit and play with the pups. It is also best that they are weaned, so the mother does not have to deal with the stress.

Ready for their new homes. *Photo: Sarah Dursik.*

While I am discussing immunity, I would like to add some information that has been extremely helpful in dealing with pups who have had their immune systems overstressed, are ill with the likes of parvo or coronavirus, and having a very bad time overcoming the illness. Please check with your veterinarian about the procedure of drawing blood from the dam, or even old brothers or sisters of the pups, and injecting intramuscularly into severely immune-suppressed puppies, either the whole blood or the blood serum (which carries antibodies). I have seen two litters at death's door who have all recovered within 24 hours of receiving this treatment. This is something to be done by a veterinarian.

From the time the pups are a few days old, get them used to toenail trimming. Start with a small fingernail clipper and just trim the sharp curved tips of the nails. Do the nails every five to seven days. This teaches the pups to accept this trimming and keeps their fast-growing nails at an acceptable length. Once the puppies are outside, they will wear the ends of the nails off far better than in the whelping box, but they will still need regular trimming.

It is not a good idea to promise anyone a particular pup as a pet quality or show quality until they are seven or eight weeks of age. Bullmastiff puppies have a way of changing very rapidly from day to day. Unless a pup has a very obvious major structural or pigment fault, there is every possibility you will change your evaluation several times before the pups are eight weeks old.

Friends for life.

When you are ready to send a puppy home with his new owners, be sure to send a very clear list of diet, vaccines, worming and any other information you feel is important. Send at least a three-generation pedigree. If you do not have the registration application for the pup yet, send a statement showing the registered names and numbers of the parents, color, birth date, sex of the pup and a promise to forward the papers by a date not more than four to six weeks from the date the pup leaves. Be sure your name, address and phone number are on at least one of the papers you give the new owners. You have spent a lot of time on these pups, and you want to be sure the new owners can reach you with any questions or problems they might have.

Chapter 14

Spaying and Neutering

Not all Bullmastiffs are show and breeding quality. That does not mean they are not wonderful companions, handsome or beautiful, or worthy of a place in your home and heart. The best gift you can give your pet dog is to spay or neuter. There are illnesses that afflict unneutered animals that never are a factor in the lives of "fixed" pets.

Tubal ligation — the severing and tying off of the Fallopian tubes — is one way to prevent pregnancy in a bitch. Vasectomy, the severing and tying off of the sperm ducts on a male, will keep him from reproducing. These two surgeries will not change the dog's hormonal sexual responses in the slightest, and they won't protect him from the reproductive diseases that afflict intact animals. To my mind, they are a stopgap at best and a waste of time.

Spaying a bitch at an early age totally prevents pyometra (a massive uterine infection) and uterine cancer (can't get cancer in something that isn't there). It reduces the occurrence of mammary cancer to a totally insignificant level. If you want your purely pet bitch to have a long and pleasant life, spay her. Every time she comes in season, her risks are that much higher for a problem. She can also travel anywhere with you at any time of the year without causing a drippy mess or attracting all the interested males for miles around. There won't be any accidental breedings with the dog who jumped the fence to visit while you weren't looking.

Bitches come in season for the first time from six months to a year of age. If you wish to wait until the bitch's second heat before spaying (which some people believe helps reduce the risk of spay incontinence, discussed in the next paragraph), you will just have to be very careful for the three weeks that she is in season. For most people, spending three weeks following their bitch with mop in hand is a good incentive to spay her.

One thing you need to watch for in the spayed bitch is urine leakage. With the removal of estrogen from the system, the sphincter muscle on the bladder can weaken. If you think you bitch is suddenly doing spiteful little waterings around the house about six months to a year after she is spayed, ask her to accept your apology. She is as surprised as you. The normal scenario is for the bitch to take a nap, and while she is relaxed in sleep, her bladder leaks. When she wakes up, she finds someone played a cruel joke and

she is lying in a pool of something and she has no idea how it got there. She can't help it. You can fix that in a day or two. There are hormones or medications that the bitch can take that stop this immediately. It is as simple as dropping a pill in her food. This small effort is worth it when compared with the possible problems the bitch could develop if left unspayed.

Castrating a dog who is not going to ever be used for breeding is a kindness. It is difficult to get some people to do this, as they seem to take the whole procedure terribly personally. Neither the dog or bitch who is altered has the slightest interest in things sexual since all their sexual reactions are the result of hormonal changes that are removed from their lives with their reproductive parts. A castrated dog will never go through the misery of testicular cancer, and will be spared prostate infections. He also will not go bonkers every time the bitch on the next block comes in season and the wind is blowing the right way for him to pick that up. He will be a happy, loving friend whose life has probably been extended by several years.

Leaving a male unaltered until a year of age will probably allow him to develop a little more masculine look than the dog altered earlier, but I don't seem to find a great deal of difference. Personally, I do not spay or neuter except in emergency cases under 12 to 18 months of age, and I prefer 18 months.

Neither the altered dog or bitch need get fat and lazy. Altered animal require less food. You would be amazed at how much energy must be generated related to the reproductive system. When fed in the proper amounts and given reasonable exercise, they have no trouble staying fit, trim and active.

Do not try to give human feelings to your dog. His or her life will be happy and fulfilling without the extra baggage of the reproductive cycle.

Photo: Gwen Bader

Chapter 15

The Late Years to Goodbye

The average lifespan of the Bullmastiff, as well as almost all the very large or giant breeds, is eight years. Many live to 10 or older, but the majority do not. There are things one can do environmentally to assist the genetic influences of the dog to extend the lifespan.

Obesity is a killer. The cardiovascular, digestive and renal systems of an obese dog are severely overworked. Careful attention to a healthy diet, lowered protein intake in the mature animal, spaying and castration of pets, and responsible weight control can go a long way to extending life expectancy for your aging dog.

Once a dog is five or six years old, he does not require the amount of protein a younger dog needs. There are several good reduced-protein diets for older or inactive dogs.

It is a good idea to check an older dog's physical condition on a regular basis, such as taking five minutes every week to inspect your dog's ears, teeth, eyes and skin, and to check for any possible lumps or sore spots. Quick attention to a minor problem not only saves money and time — it can save your dog's life.

Older dogs should still have a reasonable amount of exercise. Some age faster than others and cannot exert themselves as much, but a reasonable, consistent exercise regimen throughout a dog's life keeps the cardiovascular system in good condition, which can add considerably to the time you will have with your dog.

Older dogs are more sensitive to temperature extremes than young adults. Their metabolism is slower. Be sure the dog has a cool, comfortable place in the hot weather and a warm, draft-free place in the cold weather. Soft bedding relieves strain and pressure on old joints and muscles. Arthritis is a major factor in the lives of older dogs. There are safe, easily administered products available through vets and even health-food stores that will increase an old dog's comfort level.

Plenty of available fresh drinking water is important to help flush a system that is slowing down. Proper diet, regular health checks, and consistent and reasonable exercise all contribute to lengthened lifespan.

Even with the best of care, the time does come when one has to say goodbye to a dear, four-legged friend. It may be because of a critical or terminal illness, or just old age.

Whether you own one dog or 10, this is an awful time for an owner. There are some very hard decisions to be made. When all is said and done, and the facts are carefully weighed, the only important thing is what is best for the dog.

Who are you calling an old lady? This long-lived grande dam is just two months short of 13 years old. *Photo: Helene Nietsch.*

When it becomes evident that the dog is so ill, or in pain that cannot be controlled, consider that this dog has been a faithful and loving companion and deserves the dignity of a painless and peaceful goodbye. No matter how much we are going to miss this old friend, it is important to accept the fact that we can give the gift of a dignified end to one who unfailingly gave of himself all his life.

From an end can come new beginnings. Bullmastiffs tend to be addictive. Never forget your old friend. A new dog will never take the place of the one lost. It should never be compared. Each dog is a living individual with wonderful traits of his own. Let it be a *new friend*. If your old dog was your only dog and you are starting with a new pup after many years, start at the beginning of this book to refresh your memory on how to live with your new baby and enjoy again the love and companionship of one of the greatest breeds of dog in the world, *THE BULLMASTIFF*.

THE LATE YEARS TO GOODBYE

About the Author

Carol Beans has owned Bullmastiffs since 1965. Under the prefix "Tauralan," she has bred or owned 60 champions. She bred the first top producer to pass the 30-champion offspring mark and a number of Register of Merit sires and dams. She has owned Specialty, Sweepstakes and National Specialty Sweepstakes winners.

She was married for 55 years and is now widowed. She has three children, seven grandchildren and a great-grandchild. Her hobbies are, naturally, Bullmastiffs, travel, photography, gardening, cooking and reading historical novels.

Mrs. Beans has judged three American and one Canadian National Specialty Sweepstakes, four area club Sweepstakes, a National Specialty Futurity, regional matches, and several championship shows in England. In 2015, she had the honor of judging the American Bullmastiff Association National Specialty.

A member of the American Bullmastiff Association since 1969, she has served on its board for 12 years, three of those as president, and is presently a member of the ABA Judges' Education Committee, mentoring and participating in committee seminars.

Mrs. Beans is the former editor-publisher of *The Bullseye Magazine* for Bullmastiff fanciers (20 years), *The Pedigree Pictorial of Bullmastiff Champions and Titleists* (22 years), the Bullmastiff Calendar (11 years), co-author of *The Practical Guide To The Bullmastiff*, and author of several Bullmastiff articles in national all-breed publications.

Glossary

ANGULATION - The degree of angle between the bones forming joints.

BROOD BITCH - A bitch used for breeding, the mother of puppies.

CALCIFY - Become bone.

CASTRATE - Remove the testicles.

CONGENITAL - A factor developed in the process of development, caused by a non-hereditary influence.

DOMINANT GENE - A gene that can pass on its attribute even if it is carried by only one parent.

GENETIC - A factor caused by the genes carried by the parents of an offspring.

HERNIA - A tear in the muscle, allowing entrance into that opening of tissue or organs.

HOCK - Joint between the foot and the stifle of a dog.

HYPERTHYROID - Above normal thyroid level.

HYPOTHYROID - Below normal thyroid level.

INERTIA - Lack of movement.

KIBBLE - Dry dog food in the form of small, shaped pieces.

MASTITIS - Inflammation of the breast.

NEONATE – Newborn.

NEUTER - Term often used in place of the word castrate in reference to male animals.

OXYTOCIN - Hormone that induces uterine contractions.

PEDIGREE - List in graph form of the ancestors of a dog.

PITUITRIN - Hormone that induces uterine contractions.

PLACENTA – the attachment between the fetus and the wall of the uterus that supplies blood supply giving the fetus oxygen and nourishment.

PYOMETRA - Infection of the uterus in which the uterus fills with pus.

RECESSIVE GENE - A gene that can pass on its trait only when both parents carry the same allele for a certain characteristic.

SPAY - Removal of uterus, Fallopian tubes and ovaries of a bitch.

STIFLE - The equivalent of the human knee, this joint is between the hip and the hock.

STUD DOG - Male dog used for breeding purposes, the sire of a puppy.

TUBAL LIGATION - Tying off and cutting of the Fallopian tubes in a bitch.

UMBILICAL CORD - The connection between the placenta and the puppy.

UNDERSHOT - Lower canine and incisor teeth are set forward of the line of their upper counterparts.

VAGINAL HYPERPLASIA - Mass formed in the vaginal tract during a bitch's heat period caused by an oversupply of estrogen. This is a generally operable condition (during the heat cycle).

VASECTOMY - Cutting and sealing of the tubes that carry sperm from the testicles.

VULVA - The exterior end of the birth canal.

WEANING - The process of teaching the pups to eat from a dish and eat solid foods, removing their mother as a source of food.

WHELPING - Giving birth.

WITHERS - Highest point of the shoulder.

WRY MOUTH - A mouth where one side of the lower jaw (almost always the lower jaw) is longer than the other.

Ch. Tauralan Red Teddy

Sex Male
Color Red
Date of Birth April 24, 1998
Owner Carol Beans
Breeder Carol Beans
Tauralan Bullmastiffs

- Tauralan to the Victor
  - Tauralan Tartan Laddie
    - Ch. Wild Hearts Iron Eagle
    - Ch. Tauralan That's Amore
  - Tauralan Temptation Eyes
    - Ch. Tauralan Trust Me
    - Tauralan Eliza Truckette
- Ch. Tauralan Te Amo
  - Ch. Tauralan Lionel Love Toy
    - Ch. Tauralan Tommy Traddles
    - Ch. Tauralan Trottie True
  - Ch. Dajean Silver Heather
    - Dajean Red Demon
    - Dajean Golden Autocrat

Ch. Valentine's Chardonet Tankard

Sex	Male
Color	Red
Date of Birth	October 10, 2003
Owners	Kim Koberna
Breeders	Clarence and Linda Valentine
	Valentine's Bullmastiffs

- Bully Boy's O-Tay Spanky
  - Ch. Leatherneck Spanky McFarland
    - Ch. Leatherneck Buffalobull Cody
    - Ch. Leathernecks Springmill Anna
  - Ch. Bully Boy's Bionic Woman
    - Ch. Aamodt's Spartacus
    - Ch. Bully Boy's Nor'Easter
- Valentine's Bully Boy's Emerson
  - Ch. Bully Boy's Ode to Lockerbie
    - Am/Can. Ch. Briart's Solar Power
    - Ch. Allstar's Divine Ms. M
  - Hainlands Comet of Valentine
    - Ch. Guardman's Spencer for Hire
    - Ch. Hainland's Lookout Indiana

Ch. Blackjack Double Down on Bobeck

Sex	Male
Color	Fawn
Date of Birth	February 7, 2004
Owners	Vicki Allenbrand
Breeders	Robert Martin Jr. and Becky Martin
	Bo-Beck Bullmastiffs

Pedigree

- Ch. Ashlock's Zam B Z Zinger
  - Ch. Bastion Ashlk Runfortheroses
    - Ch. Bluegrass' Bumptious Boo
    - Ch. Bastion's Hellcat from Hytop
  - Ch. Dusty Rose's Sundre at Ashlock
    - Ch. Bastion's Celebration Time
    - Mikell Ranak of Leatherneck
- Ch. Bo-Beck's Daily Double
  - Ch. Mikell Ranah's of Leathernek
    - Ch. Ladybugs Handsome Sampson, CDX
    - Ch. Leatherneck Golly Miss Molly
  - Ch. Bo-Beck's Mad About You
    - Ch. Oakridge Theo The Red Baron
    - Ch. Bo-Beck's Little Rascal

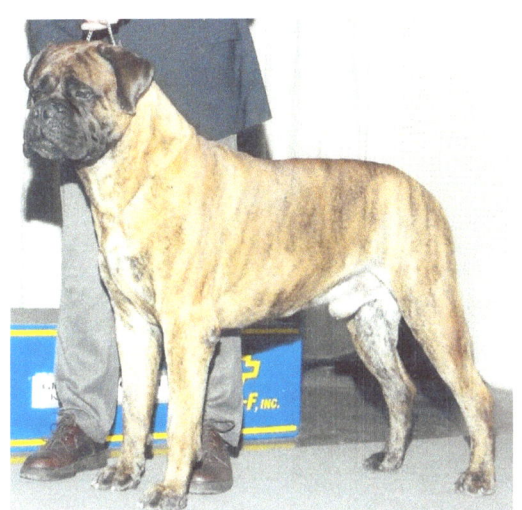

Ch. Eloc's Stormin Norman

Sex	Male
Color	Red Brindle
Date of Birth	May 31, 2005
Owners	Gerald and Karen Cole
Breeders	Gerald and Karen Cole Eloc Bullmastiffs

Ch. HappyLegs Bartholomew

Sex	Male
Color	Fawn
Date of Birth	March 7, 2008
Owners	Chris Damon and Betsy Braun
Breeders	Alan Kalter and Chris Lezotte HappyLegs Bullmastiffs

- Ch. Banstock Bruno of the Northeast
  - Ch. HappyLegs Boomerang, CD
    - Ch. Leatherneck Bit of HappyLegs
    - Ch. HappyLegs Full Moon Maxine
  - Ch. HappyLegs Winniepoo Banstock
    - Ch. Avonlea's Storybook Goodfella
    - Ch. Shady Oak Spot of HappyLegs
- Raven About HappyLegs
  - Ch. Lost Run's Sweet Tea
    - Ch. Grawel's Duke of Albany
    - Lost Run's Princess Beatrice
  - Ch. Raven's Twinkle Little Star
    - Ch. Arrowhead's Ram Tuff
    - Ch. Coyote Creek's Gone Country

Am GCh./Can. Ch. Bramstoke's Stand By Me, CD, RA, BN, CGC

Sex	Male
Color	Red
Date of Birth	December 27, 2010
Owner	Gail Painter
Breeder	Kay Reil
	Bramstoke Bullmastiffs

- Can. Ch. Knatchbull's Saxon 5th Avenue
  - Banstock Streak of HappyLegs
    - Ch. HappyLegs Boomerang, CD
    - Ch. HappyLegs Winnipoo Banstock
  - Can. Ch. Knatchbull's Raz Bindi
    - Am/Can. Ch. Onan of Knatchbull
    - Can. Ch. Rumblinpawz Sudden Storm
- Can. Ch. Bramstoke's Days of Flight, CD
  - Can. Ch. Bramstoke's Crimson Star
    - Windridge Salute to Platinum
    - Can. Ch. Bramstoke's Queen Grace
  - Ch. Bastion's Ragtime
    - Am/Can. Ch. Bastion's Music in the Glen
    - Am/Can. Bastion's Odds On Favorite

Ch. Irongate's Chantilly Lace

Sex	Female
Color	Fawn
Date of Birth	March 13, 1989
Owner	Connie Urbanski
Breeders	Lucile and Ralph Kapple
	Irongate Bullmastiffs

- Ch. Aamodt's Little Cyrus Noble
  - Ch. Little Caesar
    - Ch. Tauralan Magic Touch
    - Ch. Cresci's Ma Barker
  - Ch. Tauralan Tesoro De Azteca
    - Ch. Tauralan Vic Torious
    - Chata of Organug
- Ch. Irongate's Frosty Shadow
  - Ch. Milestone's Hannibal
    - Ch. Tauralan Vic Torious
    - Tauralan Milestone Tara
  - Ch. Danrhonglyn's Cinderella
    - Ch. Tauralan Hold That Tiger
    - Am/Can. Ch. Blackslate's Darling Dalilah

Ch. Oakridge DOX Frozen Assets, CD, RE

Sex	Female
Color	Brindle
Date of Birth	September 9, 2002
Owner	Anita Migday, DVM
Breeders	Mary Detoma, Anita Migday, DVM, and Susan Crawford Oakridge Bullmastiffs

Pedigree

- **Ch. DOX Fast Freddy of Shady Oak**
  - **Ch. Blakeslate Boston Brahmin**
    - Ch. Blakeslate Boston Blackie
    - Blackslate Chimney Sweep
  - **Am/Can Ch. Shady Oak Subtle Sylvia**
    - Ch. Arborcrest Raise the Flag
    - Ch. Danrhonglyn's Grand Greta
- **Ch. Oakridge CarbonCopy O'Kilroy**
  - **Ch. Oakridge Fresh Prince**
    - Ch. Praetorian's Zachary
    - Ch. Oakridge Dream Weaver
  - **Ch. Fair Go's Makara Cinnamon**
    - Ch. Kilroy's Postcard from Boston
    - Ch. Fair Go's Terra Beara Bull

Ch. Bo-Beck Linmor Just Peachy, RE

Sex	Female
Color	Fawn
Date of Birth	February 7, 2004
Owners	Melissa and Martin Bauman
Breeders	Robert H. Martin and Rebecca Martin

Pedigree

- **Ch. Ashlock's Zam B Z Zinger**
  - Am/Can. Ch. Bastion Ashlk Runfortheroses
    - Ch. Bluegrass' Bumptious Boo
    - Am/Can. Ch. Hellcat from Hytop
  - Ch. Dustyrose's Sundre at Ashlock
    - Am/Can. Ch. Bastion's Celebration Time
    - Can. Ch. Mikell Ranak of Leatherneck
- **Ch. Bo-Beck's Daily Double**
  - Ch. Mikell Ranah's of Leathernek
    - Ch. Ladybugs Handsome Sampson, CDX
    - Ch. Leatherneck Golly Miss Molly
  - Ch. Bo-Beck's Mad About You
    - Ch. Oakridge Theo The Red Baron
    - Ch. Bo-Beck's Little Rascal

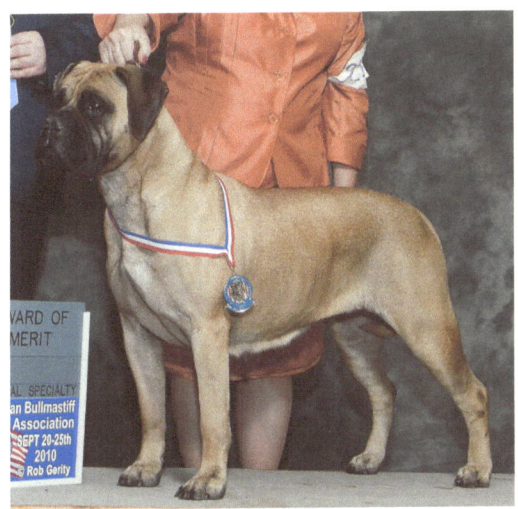

Ch. T-Boldt's Sr Corvette Cutie

Sex	Female
Color	Fawn
Date of Birth	November 17, 2004
Owner	Sherri Boldt
Breeders	Sherry Boldt, Don Evans and Jean Evans
	T-Boltdt Bullmastiffs

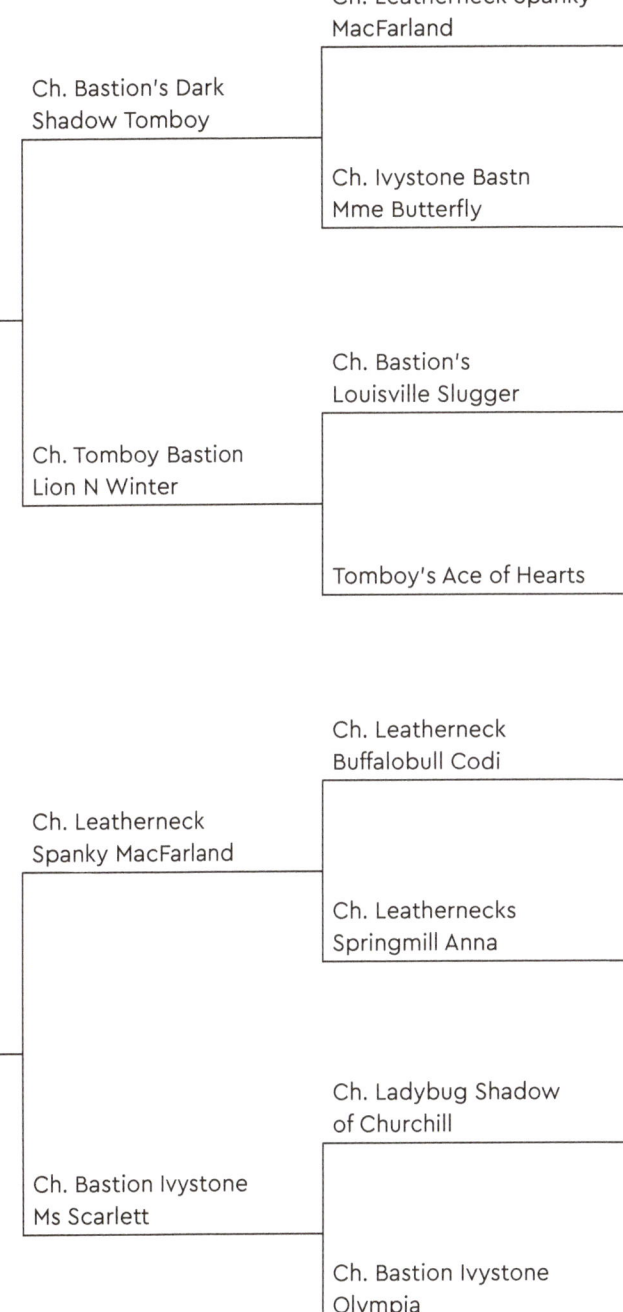

Ch. Highpoint's Taylor Made

Sex	Female
Color	Fawn
Date of Birth	July 12, 2006
Owners	Mike and Michele McGovern
Breeders	Helene Nietsch and Mike and Michele McGovern Banstock and Highpoint

- Ch. Banstock Bruno of the Northeast
  - Ch. HappyLegs Boomerang, CD
    - Ch. Leatherneck Bit of HappyLegs
    - Ch. HappyLegs Full Moon Maxine
  - Ch. HappyLegs Winniepoo Banstock
    - Ch. Avonlea's Storybook Goodfella
    - Ch. Shady Oak Spot of HappyLegs
- Can. Ch. DOX Something Wicked This Way Comes
  - Ch. DOX Arbutus of Moniaive, CD
    - Am/Can. Ch. DOX Fast Freddy of Shady Oak
    - Ch. DOX Weekend in Madison
  - Ch. Jeikridge DOX Canadian Sunset
    - Ch. DOX Burnham Up
    - Jeikridge in a Long Black Veil

Ch. Clover City's Sent From Angels, RA, NJP, AXP, CGC

Sex	Female
Color	Red Brindle
Date of Birth	August 11, 2009
Owners	Valerie, Richard and Sandra Potratz
Breeders	Valerie, Richard and Sandra Potratz
	Clover City Bullmastiffs

- Can. Ch. Knatchbull's Tavian
  - Banstock Streak of HappyLegs
    - Ch. HappyLegs Boomerang, CD
    - Ch. HappyLegs Winniepoo Banstock
  - Can. Ch. Knatchbull's Tameka
    - Am/Can. Ch. Onan of Knatchbull
    - Can. Ch. Knatchbull's Raz Bindi
- Am/Can. Ch. Clover City's Angel of Aslan, CD
  - Ch. Tauralan Red Teddy
    - Tauralan to the Victor
    - Ch. Tauralan Te Amo
  - Am/Can. Ch. Bullspirit's True Archangel, CD, RN
    - Am/Can. Ch. Hainlands Gabriele Diarcangelo
    - Can. Ch. Lady Face of the Forrest Rangers

OTHER QUALITY DOG BOOKS FROM REVODANA PUBLISHING

Little Kids and Their Big Dogs by Andy Seliverstoff

The Afghan Hound: Conversations with the Breed's Pioneers, *edited by Francine Reisman*

The Best of Babbie: The Wicked Wisdom of Babbie Tongren, the Afghan Hound's Greatest Wit by Ruth "Babbie" Tongren

The Leonberger: A Comprehensive Guide to the Lion King of Breeds by Caroline Bliss-Isberg

The Official Book of the Neapolitan Mastiff by Sherilyn Allen, VMD

Your Rhodesian Ridgeback Puppy: The Ultimate Guide to Finding, Rearing and Appreciating the Best Companion Dog in the World by Denise Flaim

100 Memorable Rhodesian Ridgeback Moments by Denise Flaim

CHILDREN'S BOOKS

Peyton Goes to the Dog Show by Lee Canalizo, with illustrations by Martial Robin

How the Rhodesian Ridgeback Got Its Ridge by Denise Flaim

Available at RevodanaPublishing.com, Amazon.com and BarnesandNoble.com

www.ingramcontent.com/pod-product-compliance
Lightning Source LLC
Chambersburg PA
CBHW050759110526
44588CB00003B/58